100 LITURGICAL HOMILIES

Placid Murray OSB
Monk of Glenstal

100 Liturgical Homilies

Body of ivory, and veins of sapphire blue

the columba press

the columba press
93, The Rise, Mount Merrion, Blackrock, Co. Dublin, Ireland.

First edition 1988
Cover by Bill Bolger
Origination by Typeform Ltd, Dublin
Printed in Ireland

ISBN: 0 948183 55 1

Imprimi Potest
+ Celestine Cullen OSB
19.10.87

Nihil Obstat
Jerome Curtin
Imprimatur
+ Joseph A. Carroll
Bishop of Questoriana
Dublin Diocesan Administrator
16.12.87

The quotation on the cover and title page is taken from the Knox
translation of *The Song of Songs 5:14*

Dedicated
to the memory of
Canon J G McGarry

A Debt repayed

Contents

Advent — Ephiphany

Introduction

These homilies were preached over a number of years, chiefly in my turn as preacher, at the Sunday Conventual Mass in Glenstal Abbey. A certain note of silent expectancy awaits the homilist on these occasions.

Within the brief compass of a single page, a certain pattern of thought has tended to emerge: starting from a word of the day's Gospel, passing on to a lived experience, finding this expressed in the verse of a psalm, with echoes of St Ambrose, Newman, St Augustine or St Francis de Sales, an attempt is made to state clearly a principle of Christian holiness, ending with the briefest of exhortations.

Several friends prevailed on me to publish the homilies. For my own part, I have always felt that the 'preaching' was the 'publishing'.

Two friends of our monastic community gave considerable help in the preparation of the typescript: Sr Bríd Cahill of Mary Immaculate College, Limerick, typed the final copy, while Brigid O'Connor of Ballycastle collated the originals.

Glenstal Abbey,
Feast of St Luke, 1987

1 His Coming and our Death

First Sunday of Advent, Year A

> Death was never of God's fashioning;
> not for his pleasure does life cease to be (Knox)
> He created all things that they might have being . . .
> Death is not king on earth. (Wisdom 1:13-14, NEB)

We know that ever since the Feast of the Transfiguration 1945, collective, instantaneous death has become a fact that we have to reckon with. For it was on that day, when the Church was celebrating the Transfiguration of the Lord, that man chose to celebrate the annihilation of his fellow-men. The sixth of August 1945 was the day of doom in Hiroshima.

Seen from the point of view of faith, the threat of nuclear death is not robbed of its terrors, but it can be given a meaning. It puts into sharp focus an aspect of our Lord's teaching which otherwise might seem irrelevant. To watch for the signs of Christ's return to claim his full kingdom might seem a waste of time, if an endless future stretched out ahead of us. The coming of the end is now within the power of men; the coming of the Lord has been predicted for such a time as this.

At our Lord's first coming on earth, a great peace, the peace of the Roman Empire, *pax romana,* as they proudly called it, bound many peoples into one vast commonwealth. Christianity shot around these lands like a fast-growing plant, took root there, withstood persecutions, and spread from Europe to the world.

Our Lord himself predicted wars and rumours of wars for his second coming. And as he was born in a single hour, and redeemed us in the course of a single day, so he tells us his return will be in a flash. He urges ut to think, not so much of our death, as of his return. And while we pray *Thy Kingdom come,* let us pray too that mankind will not unleash collective death on itself: this would be the trial, the ultimate temptation under which our faith might give way. Let us pray to the Father then in this season of Advent: Thy Kingdom come . . . but let us pray even more earnestly: Lead us not into temptation.

2 Judgement
Second Sunday of Advent, Year A

Today's Gospel speaks, not of the coming of Christmas, but of the coming of Judgement. In the Gospel we do not hear our Lord himself speaking; we do not hear any words from his own lips. Instead we are urged to get ready for his coming as our Judge.

He is pictured in two ways: he will baptize us with the Holy Spirit and with fire. He has a flail in his hand to beat out the chaff from the good grains of wheat. The first is to burn away our sins; the flail will separate the good people from the bad. And all this is told us by John the Baptist, himself a stern figure even in his very dress and food.

What can we say to God when we hear such a severe message? The best prayer we can make is one of repentance:

From my sins turn away your face
and blot out all my guilt.

A pure heart create for me, O God,
put a steadfast spirit within me.
Do not cast me away from your presence,
nor deprive me of your holy spirit. (Ps.50:11-13,Grail)

Nor deprive me of your Holy Spirit. This is what will give us confidence on the Day of Judgement. 'In that solemn hour we shall have, if we be His, the inward support of His Spirit, carrying us on towards Him, and witnessing with our spirits that we are children of God . . . That Spirit is granted to us here; and if we yield ourselves to His gracious influences, so that He draws up our thoughts and wills to heavenly things, and becomes one with us, He will assuredly be in us at the Day of Judgement . . . Gifted with that supernatural strength, we may be able to lift up our eyes to our Judge when He looks on us, and look on Him in turn, though with deep awe, yet without confusion of face, as if in consciousness of innocence.'

(Newman, *Parochial and Plain Sermons,* V,Sermon 4,p.57)

3 Omnibus Dico: Vigilate
First Sunday of Advent, Year B

Our Lord's words in this Gospel may seem a somewhat stern preparation for Christmas. As you know, today is the first Sunday of Advent, and from now on to Christmas, all the prayers of Mass have a special flavour about them.

That flavour is bitter-sweet. Schoolchildren look forward to the Christmas holidays; young adults look forward to Christmas parties. The underlying assumption is 'relax! enjoy this season.' The Church however has something different to say to us about this season. One of the prayers runs: Grant, almighty God, that looking forward in faith to the feast of our Lord's birth, we may feel all the happiness our Saviour brings, and celebrate his coming with unfailing joy.

The keyword of the Church's season of Advent is not 'Relax' but 'Be on the watch.' When we are on the watch, we cannot fully relax: there is something, someone still missing, we are waiting for them to come: our ears are listening for a knock on the door, our eyes are roving beyond the people we see immediately around us, on the look-out for that other person to turn up.

Another prayer of this season bears out our Lord's command about watching. It says:

> Give us the grace, Lord,
> to be ever on the watch for Christ, your Son.
> When he comes and knocks at our door,
> let him find us alert in prayer,
> joyfully proclaiming his glory. (Advent Week 1, Monday)

The world of business has taken hold of our Christian feast of Christmas and commercialized it. Let us take cool stock of what this commercialized Christmas offers; let us be on the watch; let us put Christ's birth, Christ's second coming first in our thoughts. Using what the Church teaches us, and remembering our own family good sense, let us restore the true meaning to Christmas and to Advent. Advent means a 'coming.' Who is coming? Not Santa Claus in the department store but Christ on the clouds of heaven.

16

4 Gaudete Sunday

Year B

A note of joy and hope rings out loud and clear in this Sunday's Mass. Joy and hope are very necessary for us all at present, because anxiety and insecurity weigh heavily on every family this year.

The psalmist encourages us:

Glorify the Lord with me
Together let us praise his name.
I sought the Lord and he answered me;
From all my terrors he set me free.

Look towards him and be radiant;
Let your faces not be abashed.
This poor man called; the Lord heard him
and rescued him from all his distress. (Ps.33:4-7 Grail)

Saint John the Baptist is our great teacher at this time of the year: he urges us to look to Christ, the Light of the world, to shed light and hope on our lives. He also urges us to prepare the ways of justice and of peace for his coming. Saint Luke tells us that when the people asked John what then they were to do in order to prepare for Christ, he gave them severely practical advice about their daily life.

The prophet Isaiah is our other great teacher in Advent: we heard his words in the first reading promising 'liberty to captives, freedom to those in prison.'

Let each of us look closely into his or her own life. We shall surely discover there some captivity or other we brought on ourselves; some chain we have forged for ourselves by our sins.

Let this be our task for the days between this and Christmas. Let us shake off those bonds of sin; let us look to Christ for strength and light. Then in a calm and tranquil spirit, we shall be able to enthrone Christ as Lord in our hearts. As we pray for the coming of God's kingdom, we shall be able to pray more confidently for all our needs, particularly our anxieties at present about our livelihood. We shall believe that Jesus comes this year, like every year, 'to proclaim a year of favour from the Lord.'

5 Gaudete Sunday:
A Meditated Collect

The wish of this season is, naturally, a 'happy' Christmas and that is what we have prayed for in today's Mass:

> Grant, Lord, that looking forward in faith
> to the feast of our Lord's birth,
> we may feel all the happiness our Saviour brings,
> and celebrate his coming with unfailing joy.

'To feel' all the happiness our Saviour brings.' In his birth in Bethlehem, Jesus comes among us from on high; but he comes, to all appearances as one of ourselves. He is our brother by his birth from the Virgin Mary. He is our Friend whom we have known from childhood, though we have never seen him. He makes us his brothers and sisters by our Baptism, and by the continued offering of himself in Mass to his Father, and giving himself to us as our food in communion.

His love surrounds and supports us from our birth to our coffin – and beyond.

Let us practise some private reflection on all this mystery of love. It will be our best preparation for Christmas: we will look forward *in faith* to the feast of our Lord's birth.

This will bring us joy. The joy our faith gives us is something quite different from the fun that goes on all around us at Christmas. This is all right up to a certain point; but after that point it becomes an intrusion into privacy, it can become offensive, whereas Christian joy is always refined and discreet, calming and satisfying. It does not wear off or go sour.

Some families have sad memories at Christmastime, because of sudden deaths or other crosses. Let them too – and they especially – make their own today's prayer: Grant, Lord . . .

6 *Urbs Fortitudinis Sion*
Fourth Sunday of Advent, Year A

Saint Joseph listened to the angel's words; he put away his doubts about our Lady; he believed, although he did not yet see the unborn child Jesus, he believed that Jesus is 'God with us.'

We live in an age of doubt and questioning. We need reassurance that 'God is with us': we are asked to believe, though we do not see Jesus in his earthly life among us.

> We have a strong city,
> our Saviour is its walls and ramparts:
> Open its gates, for God is with us, alleluia.

These are words of the prophet Isaiah, which we have been hearing throughtout Advent. 'So we are even more confident of the message proclaimed by the prophets. You will do well to pay attention to it, because it is like a lamp shining in a dark place until the Day dawns and the light of the morning star shines in your hearts.' (2 Pet.1:19, TEV)

It would not be possible to spend one's life anwering every doubt and objection that is thrown at us today. Instead, just as soldiers do in battle, we need to fall back on some few strong points while this war of words goes on. We will soon learn to see that just as the Truth which Christ brings us, holds together in a few strong simple points, so too the attacks against the truth come from the same quarters all the time, no matter how varied the direction from which they seem to come.

Let us then this Christmas, at Mass, and later on when we visit the crib, and after that when we leave the church building and go out again into the bedlam of criticism, let us build up an inner citadel of peace and strength. Let us enthrone Christ in our hearts. Let us listen there to the fascination of his purity and his truth. Jesus himself has told us: 'Stop grumbling among yourselves. No one can come to me unless the Father who sent me draws him to me. . . I will never turn away anyone who comes to me, because I have come down from heaven to do not my own will but the will of him who sent me.' (John 6:43,37,TEV)

7 Unde Hoc Mihi?

Fourth Sunday of Advent, Year C

'And why is this granted me, that the mother of my Lord should come to me?' (Luke 1:43, RSV)

It is good for us to recall step by step the mysteries of our Lord's promised birth, his birthday, his growth in wisdom and the favour of God upon him, his temptation in the wilderness, his preaching, his miracles, his sufferings, his Last Supper, his death, his resurrection and his ascension to the right hand of the Father. It is good for us to recall these mysteries, Sunday after Sunday, year in, year out.

However, it is still better perhaps not to forget, on any given Sunday throughout the year, that there is a sense in which he is always coming to us with all these mysteries, all at once.

Elizabeth cried out to Mary, 'and why is this granted me, that the mother of my Lord should come to me?' If we prayed hard enough we, in our turn would exclaim, 'And why is this granted me, that my Lord himself should come to me?' In a few moments you will hear the priest at the altar saying this prayer:

> Lord,
> may the power of the Spirit,
> which sanctified Mary the mother of your Son,
> make holy the gifts we place upon this altar.(Sunday 4 of
> Advent, Prayer over the Gifts.)

Christ himself will be there in our midst. He is the Son of God, ready to repeat in each of us. . . 'all that he did and suffered in the flesh. He is formed in us, born in us, suffers in us, rises again in us, lives in us; and this not by a succession of events, but all at once: for he is brought to us by his Spirit. All dying, all rising again, all living.' (Newman, *Parochial and Plain Sermons,* V, Sermon 10,p.139.)

Let us each complete in private what we have begun in Church in public. Let us ask for the grace to wonder: 'Why is this granted me that my Lord Himself should come to me?'

8 Beati Oculi
Fourth Sunday of Advent, Year C

'Blessed are the eyes which see what you see! For I tell you that many prophets and kings desired to see what you see, and did not see it, and to hear what you hear, and did not hear it!" (Lk.10:23,24 RSV).

It is a natural feeling in every father's heart to wish for a son to perpetuate his name; it is understandable that a king, a ruler, wishes for a successor of his own stock; it is clear that a prophet would thrill to see the fulfilment – beyond his own expectations – of the words he had sung in prophecy.

The Patriarchs, the Kings, the Prophets – what a record these men have won by their faith. Yet they did not receive what God had promised, for God had decided on an even better plan for us. His purpose was that they would be made perfect only with us. (Heb.11:39-40)

It is Mary as she hastens into the hill country, carrying her as yet unborn child, who is the bringer of 'peace, of good tidings of good.' She is the daughter of Patriarchs and their Queen, she is the Queen of Prophets, the Queen of peace. In this, the first action of hers which the Gospel reveals to us, she shows what she has ever since done: not only does she help us when we call, but she is there beforehand, before we invoke her. She is the Help of Christians.

The whole scene of the Visitation is marked by urgency, by faith, by joy. The fervour of the Holy Spirit can brook no delay. And to crown the joy, the faith, the urgency, there breaks forth the praise of God in our Lady's *Magnificat:*

My soul proclaims the greatness of the Lord,
My spirit rejoices in God my Saviour;
for he has looked with favour on his lowly servant,
and from this day all generations will call me blessed.

Let us, in our measure, offer those around us those gifts of Mary's: faith to wipe out doubt; joy to replace grief; immediate help to forestall the disappointment of delay; praise of God instead of bickering and complaints. Then, with Mary, let us learn to go with haste into the hill country of each day as it comes.

9 Mary, our Sister

Solemnity of Mary, the Mother of God

The news we listen to every day is concerned with states, with nations, with negotiations, with wars and settlement of wars. So it is today: the world has its eye on the main chance: power is the driving force. So it was always. In these very days, Palestine is at the centre of interest. So it was, long ago when other empires held sway over the earth which our generation now inhabits.

God deals by preference with persons and with families, rather than with nations and states. And just as the daily news seldom or never mentions our own families, so, long ago little or no notice was taken of persons in private life or of their families, their life and death.

The empire over which Rome ruled kept a tally or census of the population, and it was in conformity with this census and its requirements that Mary set out for Bethlehem shortly before the birth of Jesus. She was only another cipher in the census, she and Joseph and the unborn child.

God's ways are surer and more lasting than those of human power. Who now thinks of the Roman Empire, except as a subject of study by schoolboys and scholars, or perhaps for some documentary film or find?

We know how many people still think of Mary, each day and every day.

This particular day, the Octave Day of Christmas is devoted in a special way to honouring Mary as the Mother of God. Perhaps it would bring Mary closer to use, if we considered her, not only as our Mother, but as our sister. A great saint of ancient times has expressed it thus:

> . . . What was born of Mary, according to scripture, was by nature human; the Lord's body was a real one – real, because it was the same as ours. This was so because Mary was our sister, since are all descended from Adam . . . Athanasius, (*The Divine Office* 1,253).

We know too what a gentle but powerful influence a sister has in a family. It is never put into words, but her example wins us to what is best in ourselves.

Let us then imitate Mary, the Mother of God, our sister by our nature: the Virgin most prudent, most faithful.

10 Praying for Peace
New Year's Day

There is one New Year's gift we all long for in this new year, and there can be no doubt what it is. It is peace: peace of heart, peace in the home, peace on our streets, peace in our deeply divided society, peace in our fearful world.

'Lord, *teach* us to pray' was what the apostles asked Jesus; the Church, in her turn, is willing and able to teach us how to pray for peace. She has a long experience of this troubled world; and one of her prayers for peace has been said over and over again in times of war. One can follow the five great points of this prayer on the five fingers of one hand:

1 It is from you, Lord God, that there come desires which are holy, plans which are right, and deeds that are just

2 give us then who serve you that peace which the world cannot give

3 so that, with hearts docile to your commands

4 and with nothing to fear from any foe

5 the times we live in may, by your protection, be times of peace. (*Deus, a quo sancta desideria . . .*)

To pray for peace is something quite different from talking to one another about it. In prayer, we look only sideways at the problem which is upsetting us; we look directly first of all to God. But 'God' is not just a bare name or a mere word; God is the living Father who plants in our hearts desires that are holy; who suggests to us plans and purposes which are correct; who strengthens us to do deeds that are fully just. We see that the world is unable to give us the peace we are looking for; so we ask him to give us peace: it is what we say at every Mass, addressing Christ as the Lamb of God: grant us peace. Next, we pray that our own hearts may be fully given over to God's commands: this is a gentle reminder to each of us to pacify one's own heart, to bring it to an undivided unity. Only then do we look at the situation around us, and we ask that we would have nothing further to fear from any foe. And the final result? 'the times we live in may, by your protection, be times of peace.'

11 You will find Rest
Epiphany

Every feast of our blessed Lord tells us something about him and about ourselves. This feast of the Epiphany reveals him for what he truly is — the centre of all mankind. The wise men came from the East to do him homage: the first of the thousands and millions ever since who have come to lay their lives at the feet of Christ.

This is what we are invited to do today. Our Lord himself later on in his life said:

> Come to me, all of you who are tired of carrying your heavy loads, and I will give you rest. Take my yoke and put it on you, and learn from me, for I am gentle and humble in spirit; and you will find rest. The yoke I will give you is easy, and the load I will put on you is light. (Mt.11:28-30) (TEV)

'You will find rest.' What greater gift could we ask for, in the middle of all the unrest, the uncertainties, the anxieties of our time?

To find this rest, we have to rise and go to seek Christ. When each of us, and all of us together, rise out of our own selfishness, and come together to do homage at the feet of Christ the King, then each and all will find rest. He will then be in fact what he is by right, 'The King and centre of all hearts.' Then the prophecy will come true:

> Arise, shine out, for your light has come,
> the glory of the Lord is rising on you,
> though night still covers the earth
> and darkness the peoples. (Is.60:1-6)

None of us is strong enough, powerful enough to be the centre of all those among whom we live. If we try to do so, we come to grief. It is not our place. Let us during the course of this day, turn to Christ our true King and say to him from hour to hour:

> Holy is God!
> Holy and strong!
> Holy immortal One,
> have mercy on us!

12 Adoration and Hatred
Epiphany

The double reaction followed our Lord all through his life, up to the moment when Pilate asked him 'So you are a king?' Jesus answered, 'You say that I am a king. For this I was born, and for this I have come into the world, to bear witness to the truth. Everyone who is of the truth hears my voice.' Pilate also wrote a title and put it on the cross; it read: 'Jesus of Nazareth, the King of the Jews.'

Jesus exercises his kingship over those 'who hear his voice,' that is over those who listen to his voice.

We must not be discouraged then when we see so much of the world indifferent to, ignorant of, or hostile to Jesus. In our own country too, we see our Lord less and less openly acknowledged as King over his people. While this is not as it should be, this is as things are, and have been. We must ask ourselves, each of us, how can I submit to Christ as my King? What gifts can I bring him? Where is my gold, frankincense and myrrh – what have I to offer?

The answer is easy. Jesus asks each of us to offer ourselves to him: to take his words to heart, to turn to him in thanksgiving and prayer, to let his peace rule or hold sway in our hearts. This is the kingdom he is seeking: this is the way he will influence others through us: not so much by what we say to them, but by what we mean to them.

If we all could make this kingship of Christ clearly felt in our private lives, then sooner or later we could gradually, slowly, influence public life. This should be the gift we could offer to our own time. *The peace of Christ in the Kingdom of Christ.*

13 Usque Ad Contemplandam Speciem Tuae Celsitudinis

Epiphany

The night sky in winter speaks to us of our Creator: all is starry, beautiful and still.

> The heavens proclaim the glory of God
> and the firmament shows forth the work of his hands
> night unto night makes known the message. (Ps. 18:2,3b)

The night sky spoke so clear a message to the Magi that they set out on a quest to find the King of the Jews. They reached their journey's end when the star stopped over Bethlehem '. . . and when they saw the child with his mother Mary, they knelt down and worshipped him.' (Mt.1:11,TEV)

Our journey starts where theirs ended. Each of us in life is on a journey. Our star is our faith: We believe that God exists, we trust in his word, we do our best to listen and obey and follow where faith leads us.

The Church leads us all on a journey each year, from the Crib to the Cross, from Bethlehem to Calvary – and beyond. We gradually come to realize that the beyond is more certain for us than the future. Our journey's end lies beyond future time and present place, beyond sight and sound, beyond youth or age. We have to pass through with Christ and go beyond that great veil which divides this world from the next.

As we approach nearer to that veil let us pray: 'Lead us from the faith by which we know you now to the vision of your glory, face to face.'

The Magi knelt and gazed on the human face of the Infant Jesus, the face of his humility. Our journey will have its end when we see the majestic face of the Risen Christ in glory. The face of Christ will be unveiled to us and to the vast multitude of the redeemed: we shall see it as the splendour of the Father's glory in the light of his Spirit.

'On this day, Lord God, by a guiding star, you revealed your Only-begotten Son to all the peoples of the world. Lead us from the faith by which we know you now to the vision of your glory face to face.' *(The Divine Office* 1, 307).

14 *Puerum Silentem Quietum*

Epiphany

What the Magi found was a silent, quiet child, in all things still dependent on its Mother.

This was the manifestation, the epiphany, of God among human kind.

The silent, quiet child was still the same in later life when he was manifested as the prophet and healer: 'And many followed him, and he healed them all, and ordered them not to make him known. This was to fulfil what was spoken by the prophet Isaiah:

> Behold my servant whom I have chosen,
> my beloved with whom my soul is well pleased.
> I will put my Spirit upon him,
> and he will proclaim justice to the Gentiles.
> He will not wrangle or cry aloud,
> nor will any one hear his voice in the streets:
> he will not break a bruised reed
> or quench a smouldering wick,
> till he brings justice to victory;
> and in his name will the Gentiles hope. (Mt 12:15-21)

Herod set out to shed Christ's blood, but did not succeed. It was reserved for Christ himself later on, when his hour had come, to lay down his life, and to offer his life's blood as the sacrifice for our sins.

This Blood is now given to us to drink; the body that was crucified is given to us to eat. When we eat this flesh and drink this blood, they are like a light shining in a dark place, until the day dawns and the morning star rises in our hearts. It is a manifestation in stillness and quietness, and tranquillity of heart. (2 Pet.1:19)

This is our constantly repeated sharing in the mystery of Christ's manifestation, his epiphany. But there is something further: In God's inscrutable Providence the great nations of the East (China, India, Japan) have not yet come in procession to lay their gifts of gold, frankincense and myrrh at the feet of the silent, quiet Christ child. But there is a continent where the manifestation of God's coming among human kind is clearer today, and that is Africa.

This is the epiphany of our time: let us make sure *to enter in* with them to the Kingdom of our Saviour, who was revealed to us this day.

Lent and Easter

15 To watch one Hour with Jesus
First Sunday of Lent, Year B

It is a great rule in our Christian life, that our Lord has been already beforehand in every situation in which we find ourselves.

This is especially true of trials, or temptations as we call them. Because he went through trial, he is able to sympathize with us, since he knows by practical experience, step by step, what it meant to be under trial.

Perhaps you are saying silently to yourself, 'It was all right for him: he could not be beaten under trial. But I feel so different when trying circumstances arise. I feel so isolated, so alone, with no one to turn to.'

Well, here too our Lord is our model and our helper. He too knew what it felt like to be alone; he felt the need of support from companions. His greatest praise of the apostles who remained faithful to him was his phrase, 'You are they who have continued with me in my trials.' (Luke 22:28, CCD) And his greatest reproach to Saint Peter in the garden was, 'Could you not then watch one hour with me? Watch and pray, that you may not enter into temptation. The spirit indeed is willing, but the flesh is weak.' (Mt. 26:40-41, CCD)

How can we 'watch one hour with Jesus?' The spirit indeed is willing but what Scripture calls the 'flesh', that is our physical nature, is weak; we recoil from suffering and pain, or even from any prolonged attention to the things of God.

> O my Strength, it is you to whom I turn,
> for you, O God, are my stronghold,
> the God who shows me love. (Ps. 58: 10,11)

Behind the difficult circumstances which cause us pain, we must learn to discern the hand of God who is training us by testing us. 'Now all discipline seems for the present to be a matter not for joy, but for grief; but afterwards it yields the most peaceful fruit of justice to those who have been exercised by it.' (Heb. 12:11, CCD)

Let us then brace ourselves for the test: it is the whole meaning of our eventual death, preparing as it does for the Cross and Resurrection.

16 Iesus Quaestio Mundi
First Sunday of Lent, Year C

'If you are the Son of God, throw yourself down from here.' We hear the same challenge, charged with mockery and hate, at the crucifixion: 'The people stood there watching while the Jewish leaders jeered at him: "He saved others: let him save himself if he is the Messiah whom God has chosen." The soldiers also mocked him: they came up to him and offered him cheap wine, and said, "Save yourself if you are the king of the Jews,"' (Lk. 23: 35a-6 TEV)

This was the great sin of the world – the crucifixion of Jesus the Son of God, amid the jeers of the leaders and under the stares of the crowds. Here evil words were put openly and publicly in the mouths of cruel men, by that self-same evil spirit, the Devil, who said to Jesus in the desert: 'If you are the Son of God, throw yourself down from here.'

This hostile, irreverent and mocking spirit is still at large today – perhaps never more than today. Led astray by Satan, by this spirit of evil, many people are again crucifying to themselves the Son of God and exposing him to public shame. This is still the great sin of the world, and we all have some share in it. (Heb. 6:6, TEV)

What can we do to rid ourselves of all that weighs us down, of the sinful habit that clings so closely? (Heb. 12:1, Knox) We have heard in today's first reading from St. Paul what we can do: "God's message is near you, on your lips and in your heart" – that is the message of faith that we preach. If you confess that Jesus is Lord, and believe that God raised him from death, you will be saved . . . "Whoever believes in him will not be disappointed."' (Rom.10:8,9,11)

To believe in Jesus is first of all to turn to him as to our model. But much more than this, it is to come to him as to our Saviour, the innocent Lamb of God who takes away the sin of the world. He is not far away and in the past; he is near to you, on your lips and in your heart especially when the priest offers you Holy Communion, saying "The Body and Blood of Christ." (Luke 23:35-6 TEV)

17 Transfiguration
Second Sunday of Lent, Year A

To climb a mountain on a fine summer's day, in the company of small group of friends, is to be drawn closer at each ascending step. The sounds from the valley die away beneath us, and we are left to our own thoughts as we see more and more of the countryside unfold itself before us. It is a privileged day, a privileged setting. It is a time of revelation.

Our Lord took three of his apostles, three of his friends as he later called them, with him on a mountain climb. 'I do not call you servants any longer, because a servant does not know what his master is doing. Instead I call you friends, because I have told you everything I have heard from my Father.' (John 15:15, TEV) It was a time of revelation. He had mysteries to reveal to them: mysteries of his own sufferings and death, mysteries of his majesty and glory, the mystery of his sonship and the Fatherhood of God, the mystery of God's dealings through the ages with this world in order to redeem it.

This explains the added presence of Moses and Elias: the Old and New Testaments stood over against each other: Moses and Elias were speaking with Jesus, as St Luke puts it, about his passing over, his death and resurrection that he was to accomplish in Jerusalem. (Lk.9:31) This explains the glory of the Son of Man the three apostles saw and which St. John saw once again, later in a vision: 'I saw seven gold lampstands, and among them there was what looked like a human being, wearing a robe that reached to his feet, and gold belt round his chest. His hair was white as wool, or as snow, and his eyes blazed like fire; his feet shone like brass that has been refined and polished, and his voice sounded like a roaring waterfall.' (Apoc. 1:12-14, TEV)

What happened on that mountain top is of concern for us: the apostles, the first friends of Jesus, learned the lesson of the infinite distance between them and him, which he on his side had bridged by coming close to them. A revelation has been given us: let us treasure it against the day of our suffering and humiliation.

18 Fons Aquae Salientis in Vitam
Third Sunday of Lent, Year A

What Jesus promised to the Samaritan woman, he has given to each one of us: a spring of water . . . that flows continually to bring him everlasting life. (John 4:14, Knox). It is not within our physical grasp or taste or sight: but it is there within us, a presence or power waiting to be sought after, to be tasted spiritually, offering itself in answer to our deepest thirst, our thirst for complete happiness.

The psalmist had felt this longing when he said:

> O God, you are my God, for you I long;
> for you my soul is thirsting.
> My body pines for you
> like a dry weary land without water.
> So I gaze on you in the sanctuary
> to see your strength and your glory. (Ps.62:2-3)

How many people today complain of loneliness or depression or isolation? Left to ourselves this is what many an ordinary day of our lives might turn out to be: a dry, weary land: nothing fresh, nothing attractive, nothing growing, nothing to look at, nothing to show, nothing to see. How different is a well-watered, well-tilled garden: there each season has new tints to reveal, new blossoms, the gradual growth of fruit culminating in a glorious harvest.

Each day of our lives can have about it this attractiveness if only we use the power that God has given us. Let us become aware of his presence within us, a spring of water that flows continually to bring us everlasting life.

This spring is the Holy Spirit, who has been given to all. We all are called to pray in and to the Holy Spirit to bring us his joy and his strength. He placed this spring within us at Baptism: let us become more and more aware of this secret within us, beyond the reach of our senses, but within the reach of our prayer and our faith.

The man who drinks the water I will give him, will never thirst again.

19 The Hidden Wound

Fifth Sunday of Lent, Year B

On Good Friday afternoon we come up one by one to kiss the cross. We kiss the place of the wounds on our Lord's feet, where the nails would have been. Of all the five wounds, that of the side – the pierced Heart – was the final one and the most telling.

This is the wound we must keep in mind, as we come up the middle of the church that afternoon. The Heart was pierced after death, and there flowed out blood and water. This was the wound which our Lord invited Saint Thomas to put his hand in: 'put out your hand and place it in my side.' Our Lord has treasured this wound even in his glorified body, it no longer causes him pain, it is a memorial of his sufferings.

For suffer he did. The fact that he was the Son of God as well as the Son of Man did not soften the blow of suffering throughout his Passion. The pain was real. The bodily wounds opened into the mental wounds: the anguish of his Heart, the trouble of his soul.

Now is my soul troubled. And what shall I say?
'Father, save me from this hour?
No, for this purpose I have come to this hour.' (Jn 12:27)

Much of all this is hidden from us. We cannot really understand why his Father who loved him, should have allowed all this to happen. Neither can we understand why the cup of Jesus' sorrow was needed to wash away our sins. But so it is.

What is not hidden from us is the fact that it all happened like this, and that in some way it has to happen to each of us in our small measure. God does not inflict pain out of spite; nor does he lay the cross on our back to weigh us down. He gives us Jesus as our example to follow: he gives us the body and blood of Jesus in the sacramental mystery as our strength. Let us eat and drink that strength in order to follow that example.

20 In Stillness and Quietness
Easter Sunday

"In stillness and quietness, there lies your strength." (Is. 30:15, NEB adapted)

The stillness and quietness of the Gospel accounts of our Risen Lord are in marked contrast with the tragedy of the Passion narratives. We feel that the storm is over, the night of death has passed, and a new Day – an unending Day – of peace and quiet has dawned.

Jesus is back among his disciples as their Risen Lord and he shows himself to them – and to us – in a threefold way.

1 He is the *Prophet* of his church. "Guided by the Gospel, let us go forward in his path" is Saint Benedict's way of looking at the Christian life. The Gospels provide us with the words and deeds of Jesus, as they were treasured up in the hearts of the first Christian generation. We need to take the Gospel to heart, each of us to his or her own heart, to plant the Gospel deep there. It will staunch our own hidden wounds. When it has healed our wounds it will grow in us in stillness and in quietness, like a seed growing secretly. It will then enable each of us, in our turn, to share in the prophetic role of Jesus, and speak words of peace to a troubled world.

2 Our Lord is, moreover, the High Priest of his Church. It was on the Cross that Jesus the Prophet became Christ the Priest, accepting suffering inflicted by men, changing it into a loving obedience to his Father's will.

Christ the Priest invites his whole church to share this priesthood; some in a more particular and special way, but all share in his priesthood through baptism. We are called to exercise it in a special way when we are ill. Like Saint Paul we should then pray:

> Even as I write, I am glad of my sufferings on your behalf, as, in this mortal frame of mine, I help to pay off the debt which the afflictions of Christ still leave to be paid, for the sake of his body, the Church. (Col. 1:24, Knox)

3 Our Risen Lord is our Prophet, our Priest. He is, finally, our Ruler. He is the invisible Ruler of a visible kingdom on earth. Today many people feel uneasy about any partnership between the kingdom of Christ and the City of Man. Let us reassure them that the final aims of the kingdom of Christ on earth outstrip this visible

world, and in the meantime, 'all that rings true, all that commands reverence, and all that makes for right' (Phil. 4:8, Knox) will find its true home in Christ's kingdom. If we Christians find that the world around us is becoming more pronouncedly secular, then it is our duty to do as Saint Peter told the Christians of the early Church: "Do not be afraid or disturbed at their threats: enthrone Christ as Lord in your hearts." (1 Peter 3:15, Knox)

> The Lord is my light and my help;
> whom shall I fear?
> The Lord is the stronghold of my life,
> before whom shall I shrink? (Ps.26:1)

> Christ Yesterday
> Christ Today
> Christ the Beginning
> Christ the End
> Alpha and Omega.

> To Him belong the seasons
> and the centuries.
> To Him be glory
> To Him be power
> While eternal ages run. Amen.
> *(Easter Vigil, Prayer at the insertion of the grains of incense.)*

21 Nemini Dixeritis Visionem

Easter Sunday

'Tell the vision to no one, till the Son of Man has risen from the dead.' (Mt.17:9, CCD) Over the last few days, in a setting of perfect spring weather and peaceful prayer, we have been given a vision of the Son of Man dying and rising from the dead. Jesus was in our midst, the Firstborn from the dead, the beginning of God's new creation.

Is the spell to be broken, just because these few days have come to an end? Are we to let this vision be wiped out by the next experience that awaits us in life? This vision has been something greater than any mere experience: it has been an entry in faith beyond the veil, to where Jesus sits at the right hand of God, guiding us here below by his Spirit, pleading for us above, as he shows his five precious wounds to his Father. With the psalmist we can pray:

> These things will I remember
> as I pour out my soul:
> how I would lead the rejoicing crowd
> into the house of God,
> amid cries of gladness and thanksgiving,
> the throng wild with joy. (Ps. 41:5)

What we have lived through in the last few days is a world where Christ was openly acknowledged as the centre of all that is. What we return to now is a world, even here in our own country, where this is no longer so. Christ is not openly denied, but the society in which we live prefers by far sight, the bustle and business of life to faith, silence and prayer.

It is in this sense that the world in which we have to live out our lives can become the enemy of our Christian hope. If this is so, we must turn our face resolutely against that foe, and defend the citadel of our heart. We must, in St. Paul's words, set our minds on the things that are above. We know what is meant by setting our minds on something important here and now. This is the inner vision which we must at all costs defend in order to safeguard the one thing necessary: the final 'why' of life: What are we living for? 'For you have died with Christ, and now your life is hidden with Christ in God.'

22 *Totus Christus Caput et Corpus*
Easter Sunday

On Good Friday there can be no mistaking who Christ is, and who we are by comparison. He alone hangs on the Cross, he alone dies, and his death is the one and only sacrifice for the sin of the world. On Easter Sunday, things are different. Christ is no longer alone; we are with him, we are the people he has bought by his blood.

Although we do not see him as clearly at Easter as we saw the Cross on Good Friday, his presence is here with us nevertheless. This Risen presence is all the more real, because unseen. St. Paul prayed for his Christian converts – and we can apply his words to ourselves:

> . . . that Christ may dwell in your hearts through faith; that you, being rooted and grounded in love, may have power to comprehend with all the saints what is the breadth and length and height and depth, and to know the love of Christ which surpasses knowledge, that you may be filled with all the fulness of God. (Eph. 3:17-19 RSV)

This dwelling of Christ in our hearts through faith does not come from ourselves first of all; it is not brought about by anything we can do. It is given to us, as a precious gift, when we are baptized. We are baptized into Christ's death, in a mystery admittedly. But the mystery is real, and is there in each one of us who has not forfeited baptismal grace.

Christ is also present in the whole Church, for the whole world to see that he is truly risen from the dead, and speaks to the world by the life of Christians.

He is present too, in the most special way in the mystery of the Mass. It is here at Mass that we learn what it is to be members of Christ's body, to have a Saviour present to us risen from the dead, who can die no more. Here his words come true: 'As the living Father sent me, and I live because of the Father, so he who eats me will live because of me.' (Jn.6:57) He who eats this bread will live for ever.

23 The Touch of Faith
Low Sunday

Thomas was reproached by our Lord: He had failed to use the opportunity given to him. He had been given the chance to touch the wounds of Jesus, not with his hands, but with his faith. He had held out obstinately: 'Unless I see the scars of the nails in his hands and put my finger on those scars and my hand in his side, I will not believe.' (Jn.20:24, TEV)

He got his wish, but also his rebuke. Thomas had been placed in the position in which all believers – and we ourselves – have been ever since that day. On the one hand, there stands the united group of the apostles who saw Jesus after the resurrection. On the other side, we stand – who have not seen – and will not yet see Jesus – but we are invited to accept their word. We believe in our Lord on the strength of that word.

We have our privilege. We can reach out and touch those wounded hands, that pierced side of Christ with our faith. We have only to turn to him in prayer to reach him. This is the prayer we can say:

I keep the Lord ever in my sight
since he is at my right hand, I shall stand firm.
. . . You will show me the path of life,
the fulness of joy in your presence,
at your right hand happiness for ever. (Ps. 15: 8,11)

Holy Week, from Palm Sunday to Holy Thursday, Good Friday and the Easter Vigil and Easter Sunday have once more brought us close to the death and resurrection of our Lord. For a few days, we lifted our eyes and hearts to him alone, forgetting for the moment ourselves and the ordinary everyday things of life. Holy Week has passed away once again; it leaves us with a task to be done. Ordinary life starts off again; our task is to bring Christ into the whole of life. Life then, need not be ordinary, it will be different: it will be hidden with Christ in God.

Let us do what Thomas failed to do. Let us set clearly the image of the crucified and Risen Saviour before our minds. Let us turn to him for guidance every day in every situation. He will show us his wounds. He will show his pierced side; he will say to us: 'Peace be with you.'

24 Peace through Faith
Low Sunday

The Risen Lord offers peace and looks for faith. The faith he seeks is something precise and clear; he asks for no vague, blind leap into the hopeless dark. No, he asks us to see something new in himself, which was not to be seen all his life long, from his birth in Bethlehem until he was raised up on Calvary.

The prophet Zechariah had foretold this:

> And if one asks him 'what are those wounds on your back?' He will say 'The wounds I received in the house of my friends.' (13:6).

This is the precise object of our faith: we are to see the five wounds of Christ as distinctly and unhesitatingly as if they were shown to us: we are to believe in them as tangible evidence that Jesus is man, the Son of Man, and not a phantom.

In the Office for the Greek Church one of their poets sings:

> see the side whence came out
> the blood, the water, the baptism;
> see the wound from which
> the immense wound that is man, was healed.

We could vary the theme of the Exultet and say of Thomas:

> O truly providential refusal to believe without seeing: which has shown us so clear and simple a way to peace through faith!

All we have to do is to look on him whom they pierced: to see him not as bare God, nor as mere man, but with Thomas to cry out: My Lord and my God.

The Lord crowns our faith with his peace. His peace is the unity which binds all into one. It is what we pray for in every Mass:

> Lord Jesus Christ, you said to your apostles:
> I leave you peace, my peace I give you.
> Look not on our sins, but on the faith of your Church,
> and grant us the peace and unity of your kingdom
> where you live for ever and ever.

25 The Ivory Body and the Sapphires

Low Sunday

In the great religious love poem of the Old Testament, *The Song of Songs*, the bride is questioned about her absent lover:

What is your beloved more than
another beloved
O fairest among women?
What is your beloved more than
another beloved
that you thus adjure us?

She replies:

My beloved is all radiant and ruddy,
distinguished among ten thousand.
His body is ivory work
encrusted with sapphires . . .
This is my beloved and my friend,
O daughters of Jerusalem. (5:9,10,14b,16b)

Christ is the absent lover, the Church is the Bride in quest of him. She cannot mistake him. He is distinguished among ten thousand. She is looking for the ivory body, encrusted with the five sapphire wounds which he will never remove.

Perhaps it is in this light we should judge of St. Thomas's reluctance to believe that the others had seen the Lord. Thomas knew what to look for: the print of the nails in hands and feet, the opened side from where the blood and water poured forth. His reluctance engendered only a greater faith, once had had seen the ivory body.

Whether reluctant believers like Thomas, or docile and ready believers like John, who witnessed and wrote for us about Thomas; one and all we are invited today to enter more deeply into this ever-present mystery of the water and blood from Christ's side, and the Spirit who carries us forward to the throne of God.

The prayer of today's Mass teaches us what to ask for, so that we may receive:

41

God of eternal compassion,
each Easter you rekindle the faith of your consecrated people.
Give them still greater grace,
so that all may truly understand
the waters in which they were cleansed,
the Spirit by which they were reborn,
the blood by which they were redeemed.

26 In Fractione Panis

Third Sunday of Easter, Year A

The two disciples had no difficulty in recognizing Jesus in the breaking of bread. Their difficulty was that they did not recognize him in the events of the preceding few days – in his crucifixion and death. They had a key to this mystery, but they were slow to make use of it. They were slow to believe because they were sad; they were sad because they were depressed; they were depressed because Jesus seemed to have abandoned them to themselves, and to have failed.

Here then were two men who were gathered in Jesus' name in a mixture of doubt and belief. He did not abandon them. He falls into step with them, and joins in their conversation. Gently he puts the key to their troubles into their own hands: he showed them how to find the meaning of life through using God's word, through the Scriptures.

These two men are only too clearly a picture of our own mood at Sunday Mass. We have no great difficulty about communion: we easily recognize Jesus in the breaking of bread. Our difficulty lies in the earlier part of Mass: the readings from Scripture. Often we feel distracted or bored, our thoughts are elsewhere. We do not recognize Jesus in the readings; he speaks to us there, to offer us a key to our life.

There could be no communion, unless we had beforehand the consecration of Mass, and the offering of the Body and Blood of our Lord under the appearances of bread and wine. But this consecration and offering is enriched in turn by the reading of the Gospel: the same Lord who once walked on earth is brought before us there in a hundred ways. The Gospel itself is in turn enriched by the rest of the New Testament, and a thousand glimpses of prophecy in the Old Testament.

When we enter the church for Mass, let us say a short prayer that the readings may be some help for us: to offer up Christ with the priest, and a preparation for our own communion. If we don't feel particularly in the mood to listen, here is a short prayer which could help us:

> I bind myself to do your will,
> Lord, do not disappoint me.
> I will run the way of your commands;
> You give freedom to my heart. (Ps.118:31-2)

43

27 *Where is your God?*

Third Sunday of Easter, year B

We may well ask: where is Christ here and now? Saint Luke, in the passage we have just listened to, described him there and then: there, in Jerusalem in the upper room, and then in that brief interval between his resurrection and ascension. But what about here and now?

The psalmist prayed:

> . . . my enemies ask me
> 'where is your God?'
> I am crushed by their insults
> as they keep on asking me,
> 'where is your God?'
> Why am I so sad
> Why am I troubled?
> I will put my hope in God,
> and once again I will praise him,
> my Saviour and my God. (Ps.42(41):3,10,11,TEV)

Our answer – and not only to our enemies, but first of all to ourselves is, that although here and now we see nothing of Jesus, we have everything of his. We do not see those pierced hands and feet that he showed to the apostles; but we have within us his Spirit, and we have before us on the altar at Mass that Body and Blood which was offered up on the Cross. When he was present long ago in the flesh, he might be seen by the eye. Here and now he is invisibly, but all the more really present, he is seen by faith. Faith enables us to walk surefooted, with confidence, ease and joy amid these mysteries.

God the Father in his wisdom has brought this about: he makes Christ really, if invisibly, present to us here and now after all these years. Any other kind of immortality for Christ would have been ineffective for his Church: he would gradually have faded in the memory of men to become nothing more than that which Tennyson describes in *Tithonus*

> 'A wide-hair'd shadow roaming like a dream
> The ever silent spaces of the East . . .'
> '. . . Why are these doubts rising in your hearts? Look at my
> hands and feet; yes, it is I indeed . .'
> Why am I so sad? Why am I troubled?

44

28 Vocations Sunday (1)

Fourth Sunday of Easter

One of the most familiar sights in this part of the county is to see a herd of cattle being led along the road. We do not often see flocks of sheep – we don't keep so many sheep in this part of Limerick, but we can easily transfer what we see of herds of cattle to what today's Gospel says of a flock of sheep. One flock, one shepherd.

Of course, our Lord is not really talking about sheep at all: he is talking about people, his people. 'There is one God, and one Mediator between God and men, himself man, Christ Jesus.' (1 Tim. 2:5-7) Jesus is by right the one shepherd of the whole of mankind; and he is in fact, not only by right, the shepherd of the whole of his church. And each single person in the church, every sheep in the flock, has to listen to the shepherd's voice.

Christ, our Good Shepherd, calls each one of us. He calls us all to the same journey, but by different ways. Each has his or her way, their 'vocation' as we say. The married life is a vocation, the priesthood and religious life are special vocations: the one based on Holy Orders, the other based by religious profession on the sacrament of baptism.

Today is Vocations Sunday. Might I suggest two points especially for your day:

1 Decrease in numbers at present, through death, through fewer vocations and through departures from the priesthood and religious life. Undue publicity is often given to this last factor at present.

There are the inevitable losses through death; there is a certain strain on those who remain through increasing age. You could pray today for all nuns, priests and monks that they would remain full of courage, joy and hope in persevering in their chosen way of life.

2 New vocations. Seen from the inside, a vocation is a very personal thing, not something one feels inclined to talk much about. But every vocation started somewhere, some day, as a small seed, through some suggestion, something heard, something read, something experienced. It grows, like the tiny fruit we see forming at present on the appletrees, the raspberries, the gooseberries. Too small to take notice of just now, but in due course they will be ripe fruit, sweet to taste. Do not destroy young fruit of Christ's call in young lives; and when you can, sow that seed for an eternal harvest.

45

29 Vocations Sunday (2)

Fourth Sunday of Easter

God has a claim on every human being as their creator: all life, all holiness comes from him. He has a further claim on all who are baptized: from age to age he gathers a people to himself.

He has a further claim on those whom he calls apart to be priests, or nuns, or monks or brothers.

This call comes to them one by one, usually when they are growing up. It is an inner feeling of the heart, an attraction to a particular way of life, which is then ratified by the Church through those who have authority within that way of life.

This is what we mean by a vocation to be a priest, or nun, or monk, or brother as the case may be. Today is Vocations Sunday, when we pray especially for those already called, and pray for all those who now begin to feel the call.

Pope John Paul, when speaking at Maynooth to priests gave us the key to priestly life. He said to the priests:

'Your first duty is to be *with Christ*. You are each called to be 'a witness to his Resurrection.' A constant danger with priests, even zealous priests, is that they become so immersed in the work of the Lord that they neglect the Lord of the work. We must find time, we must make time, to be with the Lord in prayer.' What the people expect from you, more than anything else, is faithfulness to the priesthood.'

For the contemplative vocation he said:

'Never was the contemplative vocation more precious or more relevant than in our modern restless world. May there be many Irish boys and girls called to the contemplative life, at this time when the future of the Church and the future of humanity depends on prayer.'

The Pope concluded with the words:

'This is a wonderful time in the history of the Church. This is a wonderful time to be a priest, to be a religious, to be a missionary for Christ. Rejoice in the Lord always. Rejoice in your vocation.'

If anyone here present can help even one vocation to be realized, he or she is doing a great thing for us all.

30 Non Turbetur Cor Vestrum

Fifth Sunday of Easter, Year A

Our hearts are all too easily upset, even by little things. That is why the word of God so often comforts us, as when the prophet says:

Be comforted, be comforted, my people, says
your God. Speak ye to the heart of Jerusalem, and call
to her. (Is.40:1-2, Douay)

And again, the psalmist says:

Turn back, my soul, to your rest
for the Lord has been good;
for he has kept my soul from death
(my eyes from tears)
and my feet from stumbling. (Ps.114:7-8, Grail)

When our Lord, in today's Gospel, urges the Apostles:

Let not your hearts be troubled;
believe in God, believe also in me

he is thinking of no small upset, such as occurs to us all every day. He is answering the deepest trouble of the human heart: What is the way to God? How are we to find it?

Our Lord has not simply left our planet and travelled into space. No, his journey was back into the mystery of his Father:

What no eye has seen, nor ear heard,
nor the heart of man conceived,
what God has prepared for those who love him. (1 Cor:2:9)

Let us live then, trusting in God's Providence, and let others feel that we so live, without making any great show of the fact. Gradually, our example of trust, of calm, and of peace will have a soothing and calming effect on those around us. We know our way: it is Jesus; we know the truth: it is Jesus; we know the life that awaits us in its fulness hereafter: it too is in Jesus, the image of the Father, the sender of the Spirit.

31 Lift up your Hearts
Ascension Thursday

In the middle of every Mass the priest says to us: *Lift up your hearts,* and we answer: *We lift them up to the Lord.* Today, Ascension Thursday, is perhaps the most appropriate day in the Church's year to say this prayer: we lift our hearts to the Lord, to where he has gone before us.

Our Blessed Lord did not simply leave our planet and travel into space: he returned to the mystery of his Father:

> What no eye has seen, nor ear heard,
> nor the heart of man conceived,
> what God has prepared for those who love him. (1 Cor.2:9)

Our Lord did not mount into space: he went to heaven. 'To go to heaven is to go to God. God is there and God alone . . . There are many things on earth, and each is its own centre, but one Name alone is named above. It is God alone.' (Newman, *Medit. and Devotions*, Part III,XIII,(2),2nd edn.)

> Christ, the mediator between God and man,
> judge of the world and Lord of all,
> has passed beyond our sight,
> not to abandon us but to be our hope.
> Christ is the beginning, the head of the Church;
> where he has gone, we hope to follow.
>
> (Pref. 1 in Asc. Miss. Rom.)

Heaven is that unseen world which is all the more real because unseen; all the more lasting because there is no change of times and seasons there; all the more secure because 'death shall be no more, neither shall there be mourning nor crying nor pain any more, for the former things have passed away.' (Apoc.21:3-4)

Wordsworth has said:

> Heaven lies about us in our infancy . . .
> trailing clouds of glory do we come
> from God who is our home.

The Church says it even more strongly. For the believer, heaven is next door: we have a present entry to it and foretaste of it by our baptism and the Blessed Eucharist.

32 Propositam Spem: Quam Sicut Anchoram Habemus

Ascension Thursday

This day's feast, the Ascension of our Lord, more so than all the others, reveals the secret of our Christian life: what we must do in order to be with Christ for ever. We must firmly believe, not only that he is seated at the right hand of the Father, but that he is so, for our sake. We, for our part, have to attach ourselves as firmly as possible to that place on the right hand of the Father. Scripture speaks of our having this hope as an anchor for our lives. It is safe and sure and goes through the curtain of the heavenly temple into the inner sanctuary.

Our prayer today, on the feast of our Lord's Ascension, should be for our eyes to be opened to the promise, the hope of our faith. We should pray for some glimpse of that truth, some breath from a more lasting world than that of this present world, so subject to change and decay, so full of discord and discontent, of disappointments even at the end of happy years.

It might help us to think rather of going in, than up, to heaven. For the true Christian, heaven is next door. We have only to close our eyes, in the silence of prayer, to become aware of the world where Jesus is seated at the right hand of the Father, ruling and guiding us from there. The prayer of the Ascension runs:

> Almighty God,
> fill us with a holy joy,
> teach us how to thank you with reverence and love
> on account of the ascension of Christ your Son.
> You have raised us up with him:
> where he, the head, has preceded us in glory,
> there we, the body, are called in hope. (*Daily Prayer*, 415).

33 Peace be with you
Pentecost Sunday

No words could be more welcome to us today than those said by our Blessed Lord in the Gospel of this Mass, 'Peace be with you.' The times we are living through at present are particularly difficult: even the weather, we feel, has been against us.

And then our Lord says: 'Peace be with you.' He breathed on the faces of the apostles after he had said this, just as in the beginning God breathed the spirit of life into the face of Adam, formed from the dust of the earth.

He has breathed a new spirit into us also, at our baptism and our confirmation. He makes us new, he gives us peace.

But he does so, by changing us, but not necessarily by changing the circumstances we have to live through.

This is our difficult task: to live in the peace of Christ in times which are troubled, and in a world which is disturbed.

We have to look inwards for our peace.

We have to pray for peace.

But how hard it is to keep on praying.

This is where the Holy Spirit comes to aid us in our weakness.

'. . . if you live according to your human nature, you are going to die; but if by the Spirit you put to death your sinful actions, you will live. Those who are led by God's Spirit, are God's sons . . . by the Spirit's power we cry out to God, 'Father, my Father!' God's Spirit joins himself to our spirits to declare that we are God's children . . . (Rom.8:13-16 TEV)

. . . if we share Christ's suffering, we will also share his glory . . . what we suffer at this present time cannot be compared at all with the glory that is going to be revealed to us. (ib.v.18)

. . . For we do not know how we ought to pray; the Spirit himself pleads with God for us with sighs too deep for words.' (ib.v.26 TEV/RSV)

'Peace be with you.' We say it and answer it at every Mass: let us say it with special feeling today, asking the Holy Spirit to grant us peace.

Trinity — Christ the King

34 God is Three and God is One
Trinity Sunday

The heavens proclaim the glory of God
and the firmament shows forth the work of his hands. (Ps.18:1)

God did not stop short at showing us the work of his hands: he went on to show us something of himself, by sending first his Son, and then his Spirit into the world. The prophet had said:

Truly, God of Israel, the Saviour,
you are a God who lies hidden. (Is.45:15)

But we should say now rather, with another of the saints:

I knew you then only by hearsay,
but now my eye has seen you. (Job 42:5)

And our prayer for ourselves and for everyone else, today, Trinity Sunday is:

Help us to believe in you and worship you,
as the true faith teaches;
three Persons, eternal in glory,
one God, infinite in majesty.

We use the word Trinity just to bind the mystery into one short word, 'God is Three and God is One.' What do we mean when we speak of God? We mean an infinite, eternal, all-powerful, all-wise, all-knowing, all-glorious Being. Now Christ is represented to us as such – so that whatever God is, that is He. . . . While we view Him as one whom we are to *imitate,* let us not forget there are some points He is altogether unlike us, and not to be compared to us, and in those respects in which He is altogether unlike us, his suffering must be adored as our atonement, not our pattern.' (Newman, MS Sermon 352)

To think of Our Lord as the Son of God, will lead us to think of the Father whose Son he is, and of the Spirit which he promised and sent to us.

Our religion has to do not only with daily conduct: it has to do even with God himself. We are to love him with all our mind, as well as with all our heart. Let us fill our mind with the thought of God and pray to him.

35 The Mystery is deep and luminous, but dark

Trinity Sunday

'The message is close to your hand, it is on your lips, it is in your heart.' (Rom.10:8, Knox, adapted)

Father, Son and Holy Spirit: the words are simple, plain and clear. The mystery, however, is deep and luminous but dark. Father, Son and Spirit are not three separate Gods. Nor are they merely aspects of the one God. Each of the three is fully God, each is eternal, each all-powerful, and yet they are not three separate eternal powers. The Three who speak to us from heaven are but one God: 'The Lord is God indeed, in heaven above as on earth beneath, he and no other. . .' (Dt.4, JB)

The message is close to your hand. It is with our hand that we make the sign of the Cross: as we have just done at the Gospel, as we do at the beginning and end of Mass, and so often through life. When we trace the sign of the Cross upon ourselves, we bind the Cross of Jesus to ourselves, we bind ourselves to Jesus as to our Saviour. By adding the words 'In the Name of the Father, and of the Son, and of the Holy Spirit', we twine a further mystery around the Cross of Jesus. This Saviour is the eternal Son of the Father, and through his Cross he sends us the Holy Spirit from the Father.

Our Christian life began with these three words at baptism. May it end for each of us as we hear the same words in that wonderful prayer for the dying:

> Go forth upon thy journey, Christian soul!
> Go forth from this world! Go, in the Name of God
> The Omnipotent Father, who created thee!
> Go, in the Name of Jesus Christ, our Lord,
> Son of the Living God, who bled for thee!
> Go, in the Name of the Holy Spirit, who
> hath been poured out on thee!
> . . . Go on thy course;
> And may thy place today be found in peace,
> And may thy dwelling be the Holy Mount
> of Sion: – through the Name of Christ, our Lord.
> (Newman, 'The Dream of Gerontius', *Verses on Various Occasions*, 326).

36 Alpha and Omega
Trinity Sunday

There are days when God invites us to the high places. We can leave aside for the moment the pressures of life. We know that even though in the world we have tribulation, we take courage, because Christ has overcome the world. (Jn. 16:33, RSV/Knox)

Today, Trinity Sunday, is such a day for climbing the high places of God. Let us look ahead. Let us realize that just as God was there at the beginning of our life, so will he be there at the end. He is the beginning and the end . . . who is and who was and who is to come, the Almighty. (Rev.1:8, RSV).

At the beginning of the Church

God our Father
revealed the great mystery of his godhead
to human kind
when he sent into the world
the Word who is truth
and the Spirit who makes us holy. (Cf. *Daily Prayer*, 472)

At the end, God will again reveal himself to us as mysteriously threefold.

. . . while he remains in the highest heaven, He comes to judge the world; – and while He judges the world, He is in us also, bearing us up and going forth in us to meet Himself. God the Son is without, but God the Spirit is within, – and when the Son asks, the Spirit will answer. That Spirit is vouchsafed to us here; and if we yield ourselves to His gracious influences so that He draws up our thoughts and wills to heavenly things, and becomes one with us, He will assuredly be still in us and give us confidence at the Day of Judgement. He will be with us, and strengthen us; and how great His strength is, what mind of man can conceive? Gifted with that supernatural strength, we may be able to lift up our eyes to our Judge when He looks upon us, and look on Him in turn, though with deep awe, yet without confusion of face, as if in the consciousness of innocence. (J.H. Newman, 'Shrinking from Christ's Coming', *Parochial and Plain Sermons*, V.57).

He makes me leap like the deer,
he guides me to the high places. *(Daily Prayer, 296).*

37 I stand at the door, and knock
Corpus et Sanguis Christi

'Behold, I stand at the door and knock; if anyone hears my voice and opens the door, I will come in to him, and eat with him, and he with me.' (Apoc.3:20, RSVCE)

When we hear a knock on the door, we get up and go out to open the door. We know that our guest has arrived, even before we see him. Hearing comes before seeing.

It is because we hear the voice of Jesus at Mass that we know he is there. Our faith in his presence is grounded more on what we hear than on what we see. Or rather, what we hear tells us what to believe about what we see.

The words that we hear are:

Take this, all of you and eat it,
this is my body
which will be given up for you.

'My body . . .given up for you.' His body was given up to death for us on the cross. Put to death by the Jews out of jealousy, Christ's body was brought back to life by his Father. This is now the living flesh and blood of the Son of Man, the Son of the living God. It is offered to each of us at communion: The priest says 'The Body of Christ,' and each answers 'Amen.' Yes, indeed, I believe.

All that we have to bring here is a hunger for this food, this manna from heaven, this life-giving bread. Our faith gives an edge to that hunger, to make it keen. And faith comes not from ourselves, but from God our Father. He planted faith in us, when Christ, through his Church, baptized us.

Are we going to rebel against faith because it was given us before we even asked for it? Do we rebel against life because it came to us without our asking?

No, we make the most of life, now that we have it. Let us make the most of our faith as well. Let us be ready to rise to open the door so that Christ can come in.

'Behold, I stand at the door and knock; if any one hears my voice and opens the door, I will come in to him, and eat with him, and he with me.'

38 Do this in Memory of Me
Corpus et Sanguis Christi

From the earliest times of her history, the Church has obeyed our Lord's command 'Do this in memory of Me.' *This,* that is to say: come to Mass, be present, listen, sing, pray, offer up Christ to his Father along with the priest, receive Holy Communion, try to live outside the church walls what we have done inside them.

In periods of persecution, the Church ate the Passover of the Lord in haste: the first altars were the hands of her priests. In times of peace, the Church was able to linger over the mystery, to embellish it with beautiful surroundings, telling words and sweet music.

The feast of Corpus Christi, of the Body and Blood of Christ, comes down to us from one of those peaceful periods of development and embellishment: to it we trace eventually the presence of the tabernacle and the monstrance in our Catholic churches: tabernacle as well as altar: both serving the same mystery of faith.

What is faith? It is that which gives substance to our hopes, which convinces us of things we cannot see . . . it is impossible to please God without faith. Nobody reaches God's presence until he has learned to believe that God exists, and that he rewards those that try to find him. *(Hebrews,* 11: 1 & 6).

The Exposition of the Blessed Sacrament here in our church is an invitation to our faith: to give substance to our hopes, to convince us of things we cannot see.

What form should our prayer before the Blessed Sacrament take today, and on any day when we kneel before the tabernacle? First of all to pray for faith. Next not only to ask, to petition, but to thank God for his gift to us of Christ, the Bread of Life, who is with us on our pilgrim way. The design of the tabernacle and the shape of the veil over it reminds us of the tent where God dwelt with his people in the desert. While indeed we have here no abiding city, we have the sure hope of a future one. There we shall see Christ not in mysteries as in this time, but face to face, when he delivers his completed Kingdom to his Father in heaven.

39 First Love

The Sacred Heart

'I know what you have done; I know how hard you have worked and how patient you have been . . . You are patient, you have suffered troubles for my sake, and you have not given up. But here is what I have against you: you do not love me now as you did at first. Remember how far you have fallen, and repent . . if not I will come to you and remove your lampstand from its place.' (Rev.2:2-6)

The whole meaning of the worship of the Sacred Heart is to return love for love. Our Lord is looking for something more than 'works and patience,' something more than achievement. How melancholy a thought it would be if we were to love Christ less in our mature years than in our youth. How sad it would be if Christ were to come not to take us to himself, but to remove our lampstand from its place.

Two centuries ago, devotion to the Sacred Heart was in difficulty, because it was suspected to be something new; nowadays it is in difficulty because it is looked on as something old-fashioned, just gone out of fashion.

The inner meaning of the feast of the Sacred Heart and of continual devotion to the Heart of Christ is that it is a contemplative repeat of Good Friday, just as Corpus Christi is of Holy Thursday. In a sense the feast of the Sacred Heart is marginal in the liturgical year as it stands just outside the great cycle from Advent to Pentecost. But in another sense it may yet prove to be central to our faith in the divine Person of our Lord.

Devotion to the Heart of Christ, as seen and recorded by St. John, the side pierced by the lance, from which the water of Baptism, the Blood of Eucharist flow, leads us beyond the Body and Blood of Christ to the Person of the Word – Heart of Jesus, and of infinite Majesty.

This is a love which safeguards faith.

40 The Cross, our Signpost on Life's Journey

The Triumph of the Cross

Life today is either so busy or so trivial that its true meaning often eludes us: we seldom have the opportunity for really serious thought. We become so immersed in business or in trifles that we no longer see the great road of life on which we are, after all, only pilgrims.

The psalmist said in a difficult moment:

O Lord, turn your ear to my cry.
Do not be deaf to my tears.
In your house I am a passing guest,
a pilgrim, like all my fathers.
Look away that I may breathe again
before I depart to be no more.   (Ps.38:13-14).

The Cross of Christ, and especially the wound in his side, is the true signpost to the meaning of life's journey. On it Christ revealed in his pierced side, that he is the Way, the Truth and the Life. He is the Way which explains both sides of existence – the sad as well as the happy. He is the Truth, which rings true if we only listen carefully above all the other voices of our over-communicative modern world. He is the Life which can take death in its stride, and be with God for evermore.

The time to remember the Cross is when we are tempted to complain. This is the endemic temptation for Irish priests: to complain; it is this that stunts our spiritual growth, keeping us faithful indeed, but falling short of love. It was when the people lost patience in the desert, that Moses raised the bronze serpent: those who looked on it were healed. The Son of Man has been raised up in the desert of our present life: when we look on his Cross we will find strength to continue our journey, with a sure knowledge of what we are about, where we are going. We can deepen the littleness of daily life by the thought of the greatness of Christian destiny: we can pray daily with the saints:

Lord Jesus Christ, Son of the Living God, have mercy on us.
Heart of Jesus, Desire of the everlasting hills, have mercy on us.

41 We are your Bone and Flesh
Christ the King

Then all the tribes of Israel came to David at Hebron, and said: 'Behold, we are your bone and flesh . . .' The Lord said to you, 'You shall be shepherd of my people Israel, and you shall be prince over Israel . . .' and they anointed David king over Israel. (2 Sam 5:1-2).

Jesus, the Son of David was crucified under a placard which proclaimed him to be 'King of the Jews.' And why not? 'They were his bone and flesh.' Jesus entered his kingdom after he had been taken down from the cross, was buried and rose again. Ever since that day, from his place at the Father's right hand, he has been gathering a kingdom from out of this world. He has been casting a net into the turbulent seas; he has been sowing seed in the wide plains of human history; he has hidden a pearl of great price deep in this world's field.

We must not be dismayed if the world at large seems to go on its way, avoiding Christ's net, trampling down his field and neglecting his treasure.

This has always been the trial of faith for Christ's followers: appearances seem to go against them. Never more so than today, when Christ's gentle voice is shouted down in the babble of tongues all round us.

We must not be afraid of appearances. Each one of us really knows people from close by; we know that today, as yesterday, many a conscience listens quietly to Christ's voice: many a heart is seeking his treasure, their deepest wish to be gathered by Christ into God's harvest, to be found in God's catch.

> In iothlainn Dé go dtugtar sinn
> I líonta Dé go gcastar sinn.

During the rest of this Mass, let us keep our minds on the stretch, as if we had already reached that great day when the final catch is landed, the last harvest brought home.

> The waters have lifted up, O Lord,
> The waters have lifted up their voice,
> The waters have lifted up their thunder.
> Greater than the roar of mighty waters,
> more glorious than the surgings of the sea,
> The Lord is glorious on high. (Ps 92:3-4)

42 The Second Kingdom
Christ the King

'And his Kingdom will have no end.' We might be tempted to disbelieve this article of the Creed, when we hear the daily news of troubles of every sort, becoming daily more serious. Nevertheless, we continue to re-affirm our act of faith every Sunday when we say:

He will come again in glory to judge the living and the dead, and his kingdom will have no end.

We ourselves are part of our Lord's kingdom on earth. We are members of his Church. His Church is a kingdom within a kingdom: it is a second kingdom set up within mankind, and is a proof or sign of salvation to mankind. God's providence rules over the whole of mankind, as it does over the whole world of nature. But his Church, the Church of his Son Jesus, is a special people or body or kingdom set apart for God's special purposes. And within that kingdom, our Lord is king. In the words of the preface of today's Mass:

As king he claims dominion over all creation
that he may present to you, his almighty Father,
an eternal and universal kingdom:
a kingdom of truth and life,
a kingdom of holiness and grace,
a kingdom of justice, love and peace.

But, in fact, as the Epistle to the Hebrews tells us, we do not yet see all things in subjection to Jesus. (2:8) This is where our part comes into play; we must enthrone Christ as Lord in our hearts, we should pray to him every day:

Attend to the sound of my cries,
My King and my God.
It is you whom I invoke, O Lord,
In the morning you hear me;
In the morning I offer you my prayer,
watching and waiting. (Ps 5:3)

Saint Benedict invites his monks 'to do battle in the service of the Lord Christ, the true King.' If we accustom ourselves to see our life as the service of our King, we shall feel strength coming down to us from him, we shall continue to hope for his kingdom of justice, love and peace, a kingdom which will have no end.

43 Ego in hoc Natus Sum
Christ the King

When we see someone who does something brilliantly and yet simply, we say of him 'as to the manner born.' It almost could not be otherwise.

Our Lord claims to be king, as to the manner born. His kingdom is not one of compulsion, nevertheless it is one of obedience 'every one who is of the truth hears my voice.' (Jn 18:37).

Our obedience to Christ today should take the form of submitting our thoughts to him. St Paul says:

> We destroy arguments and every proud obstacle
> to the knowledge of God, and take every
> thought captive to obey Christ. (2Cor.10:5, RSV)

We have to capture our thoughts, make prisoners of them, and bring them to lay them before Christ, so that he can truly set use free. From early childhood, our Catholic tradition has instilled into us to do this with all thoughts against purity. And rightly so.

But there are many other fields where enemy thoughts are running – and sometimes raging – in our hearts: these too we have to bring under the sway of Christ our King. The Kingdom of truth where Christ reigns covers the whole of life. And not least our daily work. This is the great sphere of lay people: they are present at work, where the clergy are not, and cannot be. Our present Holy Father has told us:

> '. . . human work is *a key*, probably *the essential key,* to the whole social question.' (*Laborem exercens*, CTS, 1981,12)

We have to find a key to the problem of work, not only to give employment so that people can have wages; but to give work to human beings, so that life can have a meaning. Work is for people to do, people are not there just to do work.

If we could, each in our own small way, use this key to unravel the confused and disturbed pattern of money and work in which we live, the face of Christ would begin to be seen again on weekdays – workdays – and after a fulfilled life each of us could go to our final rest saying with Jesus:

> I glorified thee on earth, having accomplished the work thou gavest me to do. (Jn.17:4)

Sundays through the year

44 Venite et Videte
Sunday 2, Year A

'Come and see.' The two disciples had already set out to catch up on Jesus: he had not spoken a word to them so far. And now he turns and faces them, and asks them 'What are you looking for?' They answered 'Where do you live, Teacher?' 'Come and see,' he answered.

They were invited to do two things: to come of their own free will to the house where Jesus was staying. And then secondly to see. That one word 'see' covers a great deal. St John gives us no word of their conversation throughout that long evening and night. We feel it all in that single word: they saw, with love and submission, they become lifelong disciples.

Perhaps our own prayer to our Blessed Lord, especially to his real Presence in the tabernacle, would be made easier for us if we followed this invitation to see, rather than to speak.

We could leave words aside, beyond a very few, and be satisfied to see. Perhaps you might say to yourself: I can see nothing when I kneel before the tabernacle, that's why I no longer go there.

So it is with us before the tabernacle. We come. Then we have to use faith, not sight: like the man blinded in the war, we have to call up our other spiritual senses to sense the great reality that is present before us. It need not be a fleeting visit: it might become a turning point in our lives, a beginning of true discipleship. Cardinal Newman had a prayer of his own with which to begin a visit to the Blessed Sacrament:

I place myself in the presence of Him, in whose Incarnate presence I am before I place myself there. I adore Thee, O my Saviour, present here as God and man, in soul and body, in true flesh and blood. I acknowledge and confess that I kneel before that sacred Humanity, which was conceived in Mary's womb, and lay in Mary's bosom; which grew up to man's estate, and by the Sea of Galilee called the twelve, wrought miracles, and spoke words of wisdom and peace; which in due season hung on the cross, lay in the tomb, rose from the dead, and now reigns in heaven. I praise, and bless, and give myself wholly to Him, who is the true Bread of my soul, and my everlasting joy.

(Meditations and Devotions, 2nd edn, 1893, 391)

45 The Lamb of God

Sunday 2, Year A

At Holy Communion in every Mass, the priest repeats for us the words of St. John the Baptist about our Blessed Lord:

> This is the Lamb of God
> who takes away the sins of the world.

Because we know we have sinned (which of us is without sin?) we answer:

> Lord, I am not worthy to receive you,
> but only say the word, and I shall be healed.

This must ever be our true attitude to Christ: not an idle, offhand one, as we might glimpse some celebrity for a passing moment. No, it must be a personal, a deeply submissive attitude. We all feel intimately the need to be purified of sin; we believe that communion in the body and blood of Christ is the great remedy to staunch the deep wounds of human nature, inflicted by the wear and tear of life.

It is not only at the moment of receiving communion that Christ comes to heal us. If we place no obstacles in his way, his work begun in us through communion, is a continual one throughout the day. His Holy Spirit forestalls our foolish impulses, our passions are hushed, our wilful thoughts brought to heel, our wayward hearts are subdued.

> Christ's work of mercy has two chief parts:
> what he did for everyone, what he does for each;
> what he did once for all, what he does for one by one continually
> what he did in his lifetime; what he does in ours. (Cf., Newman,
> *Lectures on Justification*, 6th edn., 1892, 203)
> He is the beginning and the end,
> To him belong the seasons and the centuries.

Let us then today as we receive communion, do so with full faith and love that Christ is the Saviour indeed of the whole world, but that also, with St. Paul, each of us may say:

> The life I now live in the flesh I live by
> faith in the Son of God,
> who loved me and gave himself for me.   (Gal. 2:20)

46 Galilee of the Gentiles
Sunday 3, Year A

St. Matthew in this Gospel passage, repeats part of the prophecy of Isaiah and applies it to our Blessed Lord.

When listening to a piece of music, we often recognize the same tune repeated again and again with some variations. Gradually we catch the tune and become familiar with it. Eventually we master the music, and enjoy it more when we really know it than when we first heard it.

Today's reading offers us a kind of tune or theme or melody. What Isaiah spoke as prophecy St. Matthew repeats as history, and finally the Church offers to us as a way of life, as doctrine.

Let us recall the melody:

> . . . Galilee of the Gentiles –
> the people who sat in darkness
> have seen a great light,
> and for those who sat in the region
> and shadow of death
> light has dawned. (Mt 4:15-16).

Those who sat in the region and shadow of death were invited to rise up and follow the light of life. Many of them got up and passed over to the land of the living, following Jesus.

> When we say 'Deliver us from evil' what are we saying but 'Deliver us from darkness.' Deliver us from the darkness in our own hearts, until we are all light, having nothing in us opposed to love, nothing in us which is not true, nothing in us that would blind our eyes. (Augustine, ed. Caillau T.19, p.554, Sermo CLXXXII,§V).

Life is a daily journey, not so much from place to place, as from thought to thought. We want all our thoughts to be open to Jesus, we want all our ways to be in the light, we want to be among those who though seated in darkness and in the shadow of death, rise up at his invitation and pass over with him to the land of the living . . . And for those who sat in the region and shadow of death, light has dawned.

47 Super Fundamentum
Sunday 3, Year A

Christians who die do not simply pass away; rather they pass over to a new life. They are hidden indeed from our eyes, but they are intensely aware of us. This is especially true of the great saints; and perhaps after Our Lady, above all of the apostles. 'From their place in heaven they guide us still.'

One of the apostles mentioned in this day's Gospel, St. John, outlived all the others. Late in life, he was granted wonderful visions, in which he saw, so to speak, the Gospel all over again. But he saw now no longer the actual events he had lived through, but he understood in strange, powerful scenes, the terrible conflicts between the powers of good and evil.

At the closing of the vision, when the roars of battle finally had died away, he sees a new earth and a new heaven, but above all a new city.

He sees this city floating down from heaven, perfect in its shape, glowing with colour and paved with gold, full of golden light from within itself. It is a promise of what we ourselves are to be: each of us is called to find a place in its walls.

The city wall had twelve foundation-stones, and on them were the names of the twelve apostles of the Lamb.   (Rev.21:14, NEB)

This is what we refer to when we say each Sunday: We believe in one, holy, catholic and apostolic Church: the Church to which we belong is a city built on the invisible foundations of the work, the life and the teaching of the twelve apostles. It is lit up from within by the light of Christ, who is 'God from God, Light from Light . . .'

We do not see all this clearly, because we are still in the midst of the warfare which Saint John saw beforehand in his visions. In this warfare, the great weapon on our side is prayer. Prayer has power to sway God's providence: prayer has power to change the world. Let us begin to pray then for the unity and peace of Christ's Church on earth, let us pray that the world may truly see the Church as a clear, bright dwelling place of God among men, a kingdom of truth and of peace, the city of God on earth.

48 Orate pro Persequentibus vos
Sunday 7, Year A

All our Lord's words are words of peace and of life. And so too, the words of today's Gospel which at first sight seem so impossible to fulfil, must also, in their own way, be words of peace, if we can find out how to act upon them.

Left to itself, human nature – and particularly our Irish nature – would act differently. We would try to get even with our enemies, and keep in with our friends. But here our Lord's question stops us short: 'If you love those who love you . . . what more are you doing than others.' One of the psalms puts us in possession of the key to our problem:

How useless to keep my heart pure
and wash my hands in innocence,
when I was stricken all day long,
suffered punishment day after day.
Then I said, 'If I should speak like that,
I should betray the race of your sons.' (Ps.72:13-14)

This is the point. To look for revenge on our enemies, and to deal kindly only with those who are friendly to us, would be a betrayal. Our destiny is to grow like God our Father: it is by doing what human nature is unable to do in this matter, that we become his children: Pray for those who persecute you, so that you may become children of your Father who is in heaven.

Prayer then is the hidden key which unlocks closed hearts. We know only too well that there are those situations in every community which are practically insoluble by any human means. Prayer is the key.

Prayer will be efficacious. Prayer enthrones Christ as Judge in our hearts – we learn to leave the final judgment in his hands. As for ourselves, we remain in our own place, needing forgiveness, and offering forgiveness in the measure of our prayer for those who offend us. We are invited by our Lord to live in an unarmed, weaponless state, in which we turn to God, Father, Son and Holy Spirit and say in faith and hope:

As for me, the Lord will be a stronghold,
My God will be the rock where I take refuge. (Ps.93:22).

49 Loneliness
Sunday 8, Year A

How often do we hear nowadays of loneliness: so many people feel alone in life. The feeling is not new; we heard it already in the first reading today:

> But Zion said, 'The Lord has forsaken me,
> my Lord has forgotten me . . .'

This is the real complaint of loneliness: it is not that we have never had companionship, but that we have it no longer: we seem to be forgotten by God and man, a part of us has died.

The answer to this was given in the Psalm: In God alone be at rest, my soul; my help comes from him. (Ps.61:2).

And in today's Gospel our Lord speaks to us of Providence, of his Father's care for each of us. Perhaps this is the greatest thing each of us could do for the faith in our day. To live, trusting in God's Providence, and to let others feel that we so live, without making any great show of the fact. Gradually, our example of trust, of calm, and of peace will have a soothing and calming effect on those around us: we never know how far such an influence can reach. We could make our own Cardinal Newman's meditation:

> O my God, my whole life has been a course of mercies and blessings shewn to one who has been most unworthy of them. I require no faith, for I have had long experience as to Thy providence towards me. Year after year Thou hast carried me on – removed dangers from my path – recovered me, . . . refreshed me, borne with me, directed me, sustained me. O forsake me not when my strength faileth me. And Thou never wilt forsake me. I may securely repose upon Thee. *(Medit. & Devotions,* 2nd edn., 585).

This fact will take the sting out of loneliness, and make us lift up our hearts to the Lord throughout each day. We will live not alone, but in companionship with God the Father, through his Son, in the Holy Spirit. We will not be anxious about tomorrow, for tomorrow will be anxious for itself. We will let the day's own trouble be sufficient for the day, and trust in God that we can cope with it.

50 Euntes, Discite
Sunday 10, Year A

When we ask a question, we do so either because we are in doubt about something and want to learn; or on the other hand, we are not in doubt, we do not want to learn, but we want to enforce a point.

The Pharisees had no desire to learn; they were not in doubt; they wanted to enforce a point. If our Lord sat at the same table with sinners, he was defiling himself by their company: he would be unfit to offer sacrifice. Their question was only a more pointed way of showing their disapproval.

They did not suspect that they had anything to learn from Jesus, and still less from the tax-gatherer, Matthew. But if they had only looked – without prejudice – at what was happening before their eyes, they would have understood God's ways of drawing men to himself. '. . . As Jesus passed on from there, he saw a man called Matthew sitting at the tax office; and he said to him "Follow me." And he rose and followed him.'

But Matthew did not come alone. He followed Jesus fully and entirely: but his example enabled others at least to begin to come to Jesus: ' . . .came and sat down with Jesus and his disciples.' This was the way the Church grew in early times: it is still the way it grows today in mission countries.

The Pharisees did not follow Matthew to Jesus the healer of souls and bodies. Why? Our Lord hints it to them, when he says they should go and learn what this means: 'I desire mercy, and not sacrifice.' Jesus drew these men to himself because he had mercy on their sins; the Pharisees isolated themselves from these same men, for the very same reason, because they were sinners.

Every follower of Jesus has to ask mercy for his own sins. Every Christian no matter how holy has to say with the psalmist:

> Have mercy on me God in your kindness
> In your compassion blot out my offence.
> O wash me more and more from my guilt
> and cleanse me from my sin
> then in the secret of my heart teach me wisdom
> O purify me, then I shall be clean;
> O wash me, I shall be whiter than snow. (Ps 50:3-4;8-9)

Lord, I am not worthy to receive you . . .

51 *Spinae Suffocaverunt Ea*
Sunday 15, Year A

The thorns, along with the good seed, draw their sustenance from the same spot; the identical soil nourishes both. The dangerous time is when the thorns grow up, drawing all the energy of the soil with them, and then surround and choke the good seed, which then yields no fruit.

We have each of us to till our garden, and see to it that the thorns do not have their way.

We can easily see that pleasures and wealth can choke the word of God in us. It is not so easy to see, at first sight, how the worries of life can do so; and further, if they do, how we can be expected not to have worries and cares in this life. It would be hard indeed if our worries and cares were ultimately to leave us without fruit for eternal life.

Perhaps the answer lies in nourishment and growth. We must not allow our worries to grow strong at the expense of our own tranquillity of soul: we must learn to change our worries into prayer and our plans to resignation to God's will. Instead of thorns, grow good seed.

Many of the psalms put the right words of prayer on our lips to meet this trial:

Be still before the Lord and wait in patience. (36:7)
I waited, I waited for the Lord
and he stooped down to me;
he heard my cry. (39:2)
Be strong, let your heart take courage
all who hope in the Lord. (30:25)

Our Lord himself crowns this with his own word, amounting to a command:

Let not your hearts be troubled, neither let them be afraid. So you have sorrow now, but I will see you again and your hearts will rejoice, and no one will take your joy from you . . . Hitherto you have asked nothing in my name; ask, and you will receive, that your joy may be full. (Jn 14:27;16:22,24)

To pray like this will give full scope to the living and life-giving word to produce the seed that will yield the hundredfold.

52 The deep, clean soil of our hearts
Sunday 15, Year A

We often use the phrase 'to take something to heart.' We mean that something has deeply affected us: we remember it, we recall it, we act upon it.

The Parable of the Sower needs to be taken to heart; not so much by any further explanation on my part, as by meditation by all of us together. Let us try to turn the parable into a prayer, let us sink it gently into the good, deep, clean soil of our hearts that it may in due time germinate, flower, bear seed and fruit.

The whole drift of what the Spirit intends is that the words which God speaks to each of us so continually are meant to increase and multiply. We have these gifts on hire, rather than in our full ownership. Let us pray for the one great gift which holds all these words in their due place.

Our Lord has prayed for each and all of us for that great gift when he said:

> Holy Father, keep them safe by the power of your name, the name you gave me, so that they may be one . . . I made known to them your name, and I will make it known, that the love with which you have loved me may be in them, and I in them.
> (John 17:11, TEV) (Jn. 17:26, RSV)

Not only does God sow the seed of his word, but he continues to cultivate it. Jesus said:

> I am the real vine, and my Father is the gardener. He breaks off every branch in me that does not bear fruit, so that it will be clean and bear more fruit. (Jn.15:1,2 TEV)

Let this then be our prayer:

> Father of might and power,
> every good and perfect gift
> comes down to us from you.
> Implant in our hearts the love of your name
> Increase our zeal for your service,
> nourish what is good in us
> and tend it with watchful care. *(Daily Prayer,* 522)

We ask this through Christ our Lord, the true Vine of Israel.

53 Too late to weed

Sunday 16, Year A

1. There is one clear message we can draw from this parable, particularly with reference to the tragic and disturbing events taking place in our own country at this time. We might ask why does God not act quickly and put an end to suffering? But the message of the parable is that God's ways are not our ways. He is the wise householder who knows that when evil has grown strong, the time for weeding has gone by. It is too late now to pull out weeds by the roots, because there would be danger of trampling on the wheat. The householder will not allow this to be done, because he wants to save the wheat for the harvest. His eyes are on the final end of the season when the wheat will be finally separated – and safely separated – from the weeds.

2. We are like the servants in the parable, who mean well but would destroy everything by their violent remedies. God is no lover of violence: he does everything powerfully yet gently from end to end, from one end of history to the other. We have to accept his command to us of non-violence, of patience and waiting while we leave the final harvesting to him. While we watch over the field where wheat and weeds are intermingled, God gives us three clear duties to do in the meantime.

3. We must believe, as never before, that Christ will come to judge the living and the dead.

> Let the sea and all within it, thunder;
> the world and all its peoples.

> at the presence of the Lord: for he comes,
> he comes to rule the earth.
> He will rule the world with justice
> and the peoples with fairness. (Ps.97:7-9).

4. We must hope, that is to say we must pray (prayer and hope are really the same thing), we must pray that God, in whose hands all the hearts of men lie, would influence the men of battle, and turn the thoughts of their hearts to peace, so that in our day peace would again flourish. And finally, we must exercise charity, not excluding that most difficult of God's commands: to pray as Our Lord prayed on Calvary: 'Father, forgive them, for they know not what they do.' (Lk 23:34)

54 The Cost
Sunday 17, Year A

1. The two parables we have just heard – of the hidden treasure and of the pearl of great price – both point to the same truth: that the kingdom of God is going to cost us something, in fact our Lord says it's going to cost us all we have. We have to pay a heavy price to buy it.

2. What are the things we have to sell in order to buy this kingdom of God's peace? We today are longing to see God's kingdom on earth: Glory to God on high and on earth peace to men who are God's friends. What is the price for peace for us here in Ireland?

3. All the saints have bought God's kingdom – the pearl of great price – and among the saints, none perhaps paid a greater price than St. Paul. St. Paul came from the heart of the Jewish people and from its strictest nationalist traditions. In fact he had been an accessory to the murder of the first Christian martyr, St. Stephen. As St. Augustine puts it, not content to stone St. Stephen with his own two hands, he held the cloaks of all those who were stoning him, as if to fire each single shot himself. When however he turned to Christ he counted all that as loss:

> I count everything sheer loss, because all is far outweighed by the gain of knowing Christ Jesus my Lord, for whose sake I did in fact lose everything . . . all I care for is to know Christ, to experience the power of his resurrection, and to share his sufferings, in growing conformity with his death, if only I may finally arrive at the resurrection from the dead. (Phil.3:8,10-11, NEB)

4. This was the price St. Paul had to pay: the price of his own deep feelings. He had to forget his past, give up acting and thinking as a Jew in order to open his heart towards those who had traditionally been his enemies.

5. I hardly need to insist on the lesson for ourselves at this moment. How can we bring God's peace to Ireland? Well, like St. Paul we shall all have to unlearn something of our past, and press forward to the goal of peace.

> . . . The Kingdom of heaven is like a merchant looking for fine pearls: when he finds one of great value he goes and sells everything he owns and buys it.

55 One Long Day

Sunday 18, Year A

The Gospel has set before us a day in the life of Jesus: from early morning until sunset. He unites, he heals, he satisfies. Those whom he had found as a mere crowd, he had gathered together as a people before the sun went down. Those who were sick, he healed. Those who were hungry, he fed and satisfied.

In all this he was carrying out the work he had come to do for his Father:

From age to age you gather a people to yourself,
so that, from east to west,
a perfect offering may be made
to the glory of your name. (Eucharistic Prayer III)

Our Lord carries on this work still in our lifetime. If we had not our weekly Mass to bring us together, what should we be, but a disorganized crowd, unknown to each other? This is particularly true of our Sunday Mass here in Glenstal during the summer holidays: many of those here present are here for the first time; perhaps it may be years before you are back with us again. And nevertheless, because we are all together at Mass, we cannot be strangers to each other.

Jesus said to the apostles: "They need not go away . . ." The apostles, and through them the priests of the Church, now have something to offer the crowds that come to Mass. There is no need to go away: you will find here all that your soul needs.

The life of this world is like one long day. Throughout the succeeding days, years and centuries, the compassionate Jesus is still uniting people together, healing them and nourishing them. He will continue to do so, until the whole people of God is finally united for that banquet of which Isaiah spoke to us in the first reading of today's Mass:

Come, all who are thirsty, come fetch water:
come, you who have no food, buy corn and eat;
come and buy, not for money, not for a price.

56 *Qui Multum Orat Pro Populo*
Sunday 20, Year A

Those of you who come here frequently must be aware of the large part that community prayer takes in the life of the monks. Good Friday afternoon, the Easter Vigil, Christmas midnight Mass, Vespers every Sunday – all these are plain facts, visible to all. It is also clear to all that this is a kind of prayer in which praise of God dominates.

But you lay-people place another task on the monks. When you turn to us to ask our prayers, you are giving us a further work to do, that of intercession for your particular needs. This particular kind of prayer – intercession – is a sort of wrestling with God. We see it beautifully clearly pictured in today's Gospel. Nothing could deflect the Canaanite woman from her single-minded persevering prayer. She starts with a great disadvantage: she is an outsider, she is not one of the sheep of the house of Israel, to whom alone Jesus says he is sent. The apostles try to keep her from our Lord; when finally she gets close to him, he does not answer. When eventually he does answer, he surprisingly uses a deliberate insult: 'It is not fair to take the children's bread and throw it to the dogs.' The woman – we are not told her name – seizes her opportunity. She brushes aside the implied insult in the word 'dog,' and turns it into a winning hold in this wrestling match.

She prevailed and won. Prayer is the voice of faith, and faith is the soul of prayer.

People often argue that because prayer is not action, therefore it is useless, it is a waste of time. But surely this is to miss the whole point about the place of intercessory prayer in the Church's life. Under God's grace the Church has four great forces within her: thoughts, words, action and endurance. Prayer has more to do with endurance than with thoughts, words or action. So often in life, there is no opening for thoughts, words or actions: all we can do is to endure. The great trial in intercessory prayer is the endurance, the perseverance it calls for. Too often nothing seems to happen; people don't change, and situations, if anything, grow worse.

And harder still to bear: God seems to be either absent, or silent, or both. But he is there all the time, coaching us for the final winning hold in the wrestling match, in which he only asks to be beaten.

By your demands on us for prayers, you force us with the Sacred

Heart of Christ, to have compassion on the multitude. You teach us that life is moving on, with urgent new needs and hopes and difficulties. You lay a task on us, and render us a service.

For our part, we would ask you to learn something from us, from the long hours we spend praising God here in this church, even when only the community are present. 'Seven times a day have I given you praise' says Saint Benedict with the psalmist. God trains us not only to wrestle with him for favours for you; he rears us up as a Father his children, to live with him in thanksgiving and joy.

Let us give thanks to the Lord our God.
It is right to give him thanks and praise.

If we want to point out one person in the world today who fulfils to perfection these two roles – of wrestling with God, and of living with him in thanksgiving – surely that person is our present Holy Father, Pope John Paul II. We are told in the second Book of Maccabees of a vision which seems to fit readymade to Pope John Paul's pontificate:

. . . Then likewise a man appeared, distinguished by his grey hair and dignity, and of marvellous authority and majesty. And Onias spoke, saying, 'This is a man who loves the brethren and prays much for the people and the holy city, Jeremiah, the prophet of God.
hic est fratrum amator et populi Israhel
hic est qui multum orat pro populo et universa
sancta civitate . . . (2 Mac.15:13,14)

Let us remember the Pope's words to us here in Limerick:

Now is the time of testing for Ireland. This generation is once more a generation of decision . . . I ask you today for a great, intense, and growing prayer for all the people of Ireland . . . Pray that Ireland may not fail in the test.
(The Pope in Ireland (Veritas, 1979), 78).

57 The Labourers
Sunday 25, Year A

You have listened carefully to the parable, and you are left with a question: surely the labourers had a case, those who worked more should have got more. Our Lord's parables are meant to leave us with questions in our minds: they are not merely pretty stories for children, they are his teaching to old and young alike.

The whole drift of the parable is not just to show that some workers would be jealous, but that the master was generous. He owned the vineyard, he took the men off the dole as we would now say, he gave them a work to do. He gave them all a purpose to fill up the day until evening should come. When the time for payment came, he did not deprive the earlier ones of their agreed wages, but he was so generous to the later ones that his very liberality stirred up jealousy.

God gives us all a work to do, to labour at until evening comes. He gives us the strength for our particular work, whether it be long or short. We are all working in his vineyard, he calls us differently. Instead of looking jealously at one another, let us try to look on our work as a participation in God's plan. Whenever one is admitted, one is admitted to full participation. No one of us has borne the heat of the day alone: there were others there before us into whose labour we entered. We all have reaped where others sowed.

St. Paul has told us: '. . . So then, it doies not depend on what man wants or does, but only on God's mercy . . . One of you, then, will say to me, 'If this is so, how can God find fault with a man? For who can resist God's will?' But who are you, my friend to talk back to God . . .' (Rom. 9:18,20, TEV)

Instead of complaining against our fellow-workers, let us rather pray:

God, Lord and master of the vineyard,
you allot us our tasks
and determine the just rewards of our labours.
Help us to bear the burden of the day
and accept your will in all things without complaint.
Through Christ our Lord. *(Daily Prayer,* [270]

58 In His Will is our Peace

Sunday 26, Year A

Throughout the Gospel, our Lord teaches us to look to what we do rather than to what we say; to look for deeds rather than for promises; to seek the final fruit rather than the opening blossom.

The two sons mentioned in the parable went their different ways: the first revolted when asked, but afterwards repented and went to work; the second said 'Certainly, sir,' but went no further. He stopped short at words, at promises. The part of the vineyard where he should have been working went untilled, uncared for . . . He did not carry out his father's will.

Perhaps the very thought of obedience to another's will was repugnant to him. If, like his father, his heart had been set on achieving the harvest, he would soon have discovered where his true happiness lay. A great poet tells us the secret of ultimate happiness:

In His will is our peace. (Dante, *Paradiso*, iii,85).

In the case of the other son, God was prepared to overlook the initial repugnance and revolt. When he turned up for work, he found his place ready for him and a welcome awaiting him. Jesus said as much to the Jews on another occasion: 'My Father works always, and I too must work.' (John 5:17, TEV)

We all, in our measure, feel the initial repugnance to obedience which the first son felt; we all, like the second, are tempted to say 'yes' but to do otherwise. Here we have the example of Jesus himself to strengthen us: he knelt down and prayed.

'Father,' he said, 'if you will, take this cup away from me. Not my will, however, but your will be done.'

(Luke 22:41,42, TEV)

59 An Nescis Quia Patientia...

Sunday 27, Year A

Every word of our Lord's reveals something about himself, or about the people he lived with on earth, but it also has a message for us. But this message is not always obvious – we have to seek to find it, we have to knock on the door before it is opened to us, we have to ask before we receive.

Let us then ask the Holy Spirit what it is he wants us to take away with ourselves from the Gospel we have just heard. What direction can it give to our lives during the coming week?

I have sought, and asked and knocked, and I have come to one thought which lies below the surface of the gospel parable. Once it is brought up, it becomes clear – and perhaps frightening. It is this: we all need repentance, because we all have rebelled against God's messengers.

It is so easy for us to listen with one ear to the Gospel parable: we know its meaning only too well: our Lord, God's Son, came as the last in a long line of messengers rejected by the people. He, the heir, was seized and thrown out of the vineyard, and killed.

What of ourselves? Let us look back over a long life perhaps for some of us, let us listen to St Paul's words:

> Do you, my friend, pass judgement on others? You have no excuse at all, whoever you are., For when you judge others and then do the same things which they do, you condemn yourself . . . Do you think you will escape God's judgement? Or perhaps you despise his great kindness, tolerance and patience. Surely you know that God is kind, because he is trying to lead you to repent. But you have a hard and stubborn heart . . .
>
> (Rom. 2:1-5, TEV).

How many messengers have we rejected: perhaps a father's entreaties, a mother's tears, a sister's kindness, a teacher's warning, a priest's advice. How short of a harvest are we when the Lord of the vineyard comes to collect his produce. In the spirit of the prayer of today's Mass let us ask for the grace of repentance: Almighty, ever-living God, whose love surpasses all that we ask or deserve, open up for us the treasures of your mercy. Forgive us all that weighs on our conscience, and grant us more even than we dare to ask.

60 Mission Sunday
Sunday 30, Year A

The Church must not only continue to exist: it must continue to grow and expand. That is the meaning of the Missions, which we remember in a special way today, Mission Sunday.

We cannot all be missionaries in fact, but we can all be missionaries at heart. Two ways are open to us: one, by keeping step with those who leave us to go abroad to the missions, the other, by keeping informed about the people and the countries to which our missionary friends have gone. This is a great consolation to them, when they return home: they feel, as in the early Church, that we are one in heart and mind with them: cor unum et anima una: one heart, the same heart, the same soul in all. (Acts 4:32)

Things are not so easy, nor so simple nowadays, either for the missionaries, or for the countries they go to. Things were never easy, I suppose; but at least the object of the work was clear and straightforward: to bring a message of hope and of pardon on behalf of the living God. It was a message of salvation, for the next world. Many years ago, our missionaries had added a message of education and of good health – through schools and hospitals – to the basic message of spiritual salvation. The present trend almost everywhere seems to be that these means of education and of good health are being taken over by the local governments from the missionaries. This gives rise in practice to many awkward and difficult situations. In addition, the difficulties are often compounded by political unrest and physical violence.

What can we do here at home to help both the missionaries and the developing countries? We can, of course, and I am sure we will, send some money for their needs. But much more is called for. If I could sum it up in one word, I would say: *Remember* Remember our own friends who have freely gone to these difficult situations, remember the newly baptized, the sick, the dying, the overcrowded new cities, the conflict between old and new ways of looking at life. Remember the work that God is doing through the Church, and pray every day that the door of faith will be opened wide to allow all the nations to enter in.

61 Unus est Enim Magister Vester

Sunday 31, Year A

Long ago, battles were fought out between professional armies on definite battlefields. So much so, that we can even name the sites: the siege of Limerick, the battle of Kinsale, the battle of the Boyne, the retreat from Moscow. The civilians lived on behind the lines, in hardship admittedly, but not in the line of fire.

Nowadays, we know things are different. Civilians are in the front line: the line of fire can spring up anywhere, in any street or field. The professionals are still designing and using the weapons, but any of us could become a casualty.

There is something similar in the contest between truth and falsehood in the Church. The professionals (the theologians) – are well aware of the battles of long ago, but it is only in our day that the battles are not confined to definite battlefields. Any chance conversation can give rise to discussion, argument and doubt about the Faith.

What then, can the non-professionals, those who have neither the training nor the time, to forge theological weapons: what can they do to survive in this never-ceasing warfare? What theological Civil Defence should they develop? A phrase in today's Gospel gives us one clue: *You have only one Teacher, the Christ.* He himself has said:

whoever has the will to do the will of God
shall know whether my teaching comes from him
or is merely my own. (Jn. 7:17, NEB)

A great doctor of the early Church, St Ambrose said: 'It did not please God to save his people by arguments.' Arguments are the weapons on either side in today's battle for the faith. We don't always have counter-arguments to hand. It would often be a mistake to look around for them – time is too short. The real victory will be to do the will of God oneself, on the point under discussion, and Christ will reveal himself once again, as so often before as our one Teacher. With the psalmist we can say:

I have more insight than all who teach me
for I ponder your will. (Ps.118:99,Grail)

62 Prayer, the Talent we all receive

Sunday 33, Year A

Our Lord is not urging us here to make money, but to make use of the talents God gives us, just as business people use their money to get rich.

When we observe business people at work, we see they turn everything to account. No opportunity is lost to promote their interests. They are not deterred by difficulties and disappointments: they are resourceful. They keep careful accounts of their expenditure.

This is to be a model for us. Just as business people use the assets they have, we too have to use the assets God has given us to get through life.

First of all, our own existence, then our family background, our opportunities, our health. Some of the gifts we have are given to us for the good of others: these are gifts strictly so called. These are what people call our strong points of character. We have to be careful not to take pride in them: while others would benefit from our gifts, we ourselves would be poisoned by them.

Some graces we get particularly for ourselves. These we have to treasure in secret.

There is one talent we all receive; but we must work at it, not bury it in the ground, like the lazy servants.

This is the gift of prayer for ourselves and for others. The power of prayer is the great mystery. We must believe when we set ourselves to pray, that we can change people's hearts, and tie God's hands.

For he who comes to God must have faith
that God exists and rewards those who seek him. (Heb.7:6)

This is the talent that we can use all day, in great things and small. God gives us the power of prayer: let us see that we use it.

63 The three great sins of our day
Sunday 4, Year B

The three great sins of our day are impurity, injustice and cruelty. They are directly opposed to God, to his holiness, his justice and his love.

Already before we have any great experience of life, we have a keen sense of these qualities in God, and perhaps more particularly of his justice. We instinctively fly to him for refuge in our difficulties. And it is he who speaks loud and clear in our conscience about what is right and what is wrong.

As we grow older the three evil spirits of our day – impurity, injustice and cruelty – press in upon us to tempt us. And of the three, perhaps injustice is the one which takes the most varied forms: unfairness, cheating, stealing, solicit us daily.

As we grow older then, we must strengthen all the more our early God-given sense of exquisite justice in all our dealings with others.

Coming to the end of his life, Saint Paul was able to say in his own defence:

> I have not wanted anyone's money or clothes for myself; you all know that these hands of mine earned enough for the needs of myself and my companions. I showed you that it is our duty to help the weak in this way by hard work, and that we should keep in mind the words of the Lord Jesus, who himself said, 'Happiness lies more in giving than in receiving.'
>
> (Acts 20:33-35 NEB)

The whole world is in a turmoil today on account of injustice. We are in one of the ploughing periods of history: society is being ploughed up to make way for a different social order. It was in just such a ploughing period that Christ's words were first sown in the world: he scattered the seed of his word into the newly-opened furrows.

We, for our part, can prepare a harvest of justice, of peace, of love and truth, if like Saint Paul, our own two hands provide for our needs, if we covet no one's money, if we really know that happiness lies more in giving than in receiving.

64 The Silences of Jesus

Sunday 5, Year B

'Who else can know a man's thoughts, except the man's own spirit within him?' (1 Cor.2:11. Knox)

If this be true of all of us, how much more true is it of our Lord, the only Son of God, eternally begotten of the Father, of one Being with the Father, who came down from heaven and was made man? It is not easy, St Ambrose says, to penetrate into the inner mind of Jesus.

(Exp.Ev.Luc. V,43, SC 45,p.199)

And if our Lord's words are so often mysterious, how much more so are his silences. 'In the morning, long before dawn, he got up and left the house, and went off to a lonely place and prayed there.' (Mk.1:35, JB) These silences of Jesus are not just a blank in his life – and ours – they are full of instruction for us. In the last few days of his life however, before his Passion, our Lord broke the silence of his prayer, and let us hear it:

> Father, give me glory in your presence now, the same glory I had with you before the world was made. (John 17:5, TEV)

> Father, if you will, take this cup of suffering away from me. Not my will, however, but your will be done. (Luke 22:42, TEV)

> Father! In your hands I place my spirit. (Luke 23:46, TEV)

What is still more mysterious is that these silences, these prayers are even now our Lord's great activity. While we pray to him as to our God, he himself, the Son of God is turned to his Father, and urges us to 'draw near with confidence to the throne of grace, that we may receive mercy and find grace to help in time of need.' (Heb.4:16, RSV) Here at Mass, the Church's prayers are carried on the silences of Jesus, our High Priest. The Precious Blood in the chalice speaks louder than all the human words we hear being prayed or sung.

Let us then, throughout this day listen to the silences of Jesus. They will impart to our own words the force of actions, and to our silences the significance of speech.

65 The Music of the Gospel
Sunday 7, Year B

There are several changes of mood in the Gospel we have just heard. We would feel them clearly if we saw the scene re-enacted to the accompaniment of background music.

First of all, a bright joyful tune: a piping in of the clans. 'Word went round that he was back, and so many people collected that there was no room left, even in front of the door.'

The hubbub quietens down: the music changes into a solo voice: 'He was speaking the word to them.' Then comes an interruption: all eyes turn away from the speaker, up to the ceiling as the stretcher is lowered. The music brightens up a little noisily here until the stretcher is laid flat on the ground, the stretcher bearers straighten up, dust themselves and stand to one side.

Then comes that single voice again: '. . . my son, your sins are forgiven.'

Suddenly a sharp, threatening, discordant music is faintly audible.

The voice takes up again: there is no response; the voice continues; louder now, in a tone of authority and command. The sick man rises, the crowd gets excited, the music crashes to a climax.

There is stillness again, and we follow the sick man home. Of all the music we have heard, one passage strikes louder on our inner ear: that angry intrusion into what had been a harmonious, happy unison. That note of contestation and conflict will sound louder during the coming weeks of Lent and Holy Week, until it erupts into the shout: 'Crucify him.'

Two thoughts occur to me. In Ireland today, it is this angry note that we hear more and more. But contestation does not disprove the Church's claim to spiritual authority.

Secondly, as I follow that man who had been paralysed, as he walks on his way home, I am reminded of Saint Augustine's comment: 'Christ can heal every sickness, but he cannot cure an unwilling patient.'

66 Neue Liebe

Sunday 8, Year B

Criticism wounds us, puts us on the defensive. But it also opens up our deepest thoughts and feelings. In order to defend ourselves we call on our most hidden resources. Then we put into words what we might have left unsaid.

People criticized the disciples of Jesus: they were feasting while the disciples of John and of the Pharisees were fasting. Our Lord's defence goes deeper than the question of feasting or fasting. The is a time for each: his point is that the time at which they were speaking was not the time for fasting. Why not?

As usual with him, he says some of those strange phrases which leave us wondering as to his meaning. He speaks of a new suit of clothes, of a new vintage from this year's grapes, of a bridegroom and his friends.

You know that feeling the first Sunday morning you put on a new suit. It feels just right; it makes you feel right. Somehow it gives you new self-confidence. Throughout the morning that feeling of self-confidence remains strong, while you are busy about many things and have almost half forgotten the reason why you feel so confident. It supports you.

What Jesus was saying to his critics was that they should open their eyes to see the new thing that was happening. These disciples were feasting in the presence of a new love that came to them in the person of Jesus.

We know that our parents love us, and love us dearly. Yet our hearts are so made that in addition to our parents' love we long for a friendship from nearer by; with somebody less solemn, somebody younger. God knows those hearts of ours which he himself made. While he continues to love us as a Father, he sent his Son whom we could love from nearer by. It has become a new way for us, the Way. Our Creator has become our Saviour, not only truth and life, but the way there.

He dresses us in a new garment; gives us new food and drink; invites us to his banquet. We can each say to him: 'Take my few tattered years; join me to your eternal strength; Make me one with you.'

67 The Voice and Hand of Christ

Sunday 13, Year B

The voice and hand of Christ were full of power.

The voice of the Lord, full of power
The voice of the Lord, full of splendour. (Ps.28:4)

St Mark has preserved for us the actual sound of the words Jesus spoke to the little girl; if we speak them to ourselves we have a recording of the very words of Jesus: *Talitha kumi.* They were simple words spoken in the language of everyday; they were not a magic formula taken from a fairytale. "Little girl, I say to you, arise." He spoke and it happened. St John, in his gospel, tells us of this same voice of Christ:

Truly, truly, I say to you, the hour is coming and now is, when the dead will hear the voice of the Son of God, and those who hear will live . . . the hour is coming when all who are in the tombs will hear his voice and come forth, those who have done good, to the resurrection of life, and those who have done evil, to the resurrection of judgement. (John 5:25,28-9)

He will speak and it will happen.

The Hand of Christ

The instinctive prayer of the little girl's father had been to fall at Jesus' feet and say: "My little daughter is at the point of death. Come and lay your hands on her, so that she may be made well, and live." Jesus did exactly as the father had asked: he took the child by the hand. It was this same saving hand that Jesus reached out to Peter as he sank beneath the waves. It was with this saving hand that he took the loaves in the desert and the bread in the supper room.

The priests of Christ repeat his gestures and his words: the power comes from him. The words are plain and simple, whether at Mass, in Baptism, in confession, in the anointing of the sick.

If we had eyes that really saw, and ears that really listened, we, like the people spoken of in today's gospel we also "would be overcome with amazement," we would see and hear Christ in our midst.

68 Rex Noster

Sunday 17, Year B

It is curious that while the people said 'This really is the prophet who is to come into the world,' Jesus fled from them, not because they were treating him as a prophet, but as a king. Our Lord was really both – both their Prophet and their King. He was also their Priest, as he had hinted at, by the multiplication of the loaves, which foreshadowed the Eucharist.

Our Lord went to meet the crowds as their Prophet; he slipped away from them, for the moment, as their King. He showed himself later to be our King by rising from the dead, by ascending into heaven, by sending down the Holy Spirit, by converting the nations, and by forming his Church to be a visible kingdom on earth.

Our Lord's rule might seem to be weak: the world at large does not seem to obey him; the world follows other leaders besides Christ. However, what appears on the surface of things is not always the true state of affairs.

Our Lord still withdraws into the hills, away from those who would wish to see him rule in the way of the world. He would be only one leader among many, if his kingdom on earth could be numbered as one of the great Powers. He himself said to Pilate:

> My kingship is not of this world; if my kingship were of this world, my servants would fight, that I might not be handed over to the Jews, but my kingship is not from the world.   (Jn. 18:37)

Appearances tell against the power of Christ's kingdom: but this should not cause us surprise. He foretold it:

> If the world hates you, know that it has hated me before it hated you . . . Remember the word that I said to you 'A servant is not greater than his master . . .' In the world you will have tribulation; but be of good cheer; I have overcome the world. (Jn. 15:18,20; 16:33).

Let us stake our faith against the appearances; let us believe what we say in the Creed: He will come again in glory to judge the living and the dead, and his kingdom will have no end.

69 Unless the Father draws him
Sunday 19, Year B

Every family or school has experience of unpleasant quarrels when authority is challenged, and the bitter question is flung at parent or teacher: Who are you anyway?

Our Lord himself was challenged in the same way. He was offering his greatest gift to the Jews. He said: 'I am the bread which came down from heaven.' The Jews challenged this: '. . . down from heaven? Is not this Jesus, the son of Joseph, whose father and mother we know?'

Our Lord does not correct their mistakes about his being the son of Joseph. But he warns them: 'No one can come to me unless the Father who sent me draws him; and I will raise him up on the last day.' That is to day, no one will be able to see more in me than the supposed son of Joseph unless he receives grace from God the Father to see Jesus as the bread from heaven.

Our Lord's warning to the Jews is addressed to us also. Ever since the Mass was put into English, and other changes came in, such as standing instead of kneeling for communion, there is a certain risk of over-familiarity on our part to the great mystery of faith. Like the Jews, we may be tempted to think only thoughts of earth, not thoughts of heaven about the Blessed Eucharist.

We should be grateful for the changes in the Mass, because they bring it nearer to us. But each of us, on his or her part, has more to do now: we must bring an ever stronger faith than people did formerly. We could begin by remaining on for a few moments after Mass to thank God for the gift of the bread from heaven.

But especially during Mass, at the moment of consecration and during the prayers which immediately follow it, let us concentrate all our mind and soul on what is happening at the altar: this is the son of Mary, the son of David, the King who is to come, who is here with us, Emmanuel, who came down from heaven to give us his flesh to eat and so bring us to heaven with him.

70 Artos ouranios

We cannot explain the mysteries of our faith, but we can put them into words. By comparing one mystery with another, we can help ourselves to accept and love them: the light from one mystery will clarify the difficulty arising from another.

The Son of Man came down from heaven, once, long ago, when he was born of our Lady. He comes as the living Bread from heaven repeatedly at Mass. We can help our understanding of his presence in the Eucharist, if we compare it to his first coming on earth. When we speak of his 'coming' in either case – at the Incarnation and in the Eucharist – there is no question of travel, distance or space, as we usually understand such things.

The Jews had asked the question: 'How can this man give us his flesh to eat?' We can answer that question by two prayers from the Mass:

1 The bread and wine on the altar, as physical things, come from earth, not from heaven. This is quite clearly said in the prayer at the Offertory:

> through your goodness we have this bread to offer which earth has given and human hands have made.

2 The consecration of the bread and wine comes from heaven: We shall hear this during the Canon of the Mass:

> And so, Father, we bring you these gifts
> We ask you to make them holy by the power of
> your Spirit
> that they may become the body and blood
> of your Son, our Lord Jesus Christ.

This then is our answer to the Jews' question: 'How can this man give us his flesh to eat?' – How?

> By the power of his Spirit
> in answer to the Church's prayer
> said by the ministry of her priests.

71 The Tragedy of Refusal
Sunday 21, Year B

The greatest tragedy that can happen in life is the tragedy of refusal: refusal to accept God's best gifts and his greatest promises.

We have just listened to, and almost seen with our own eyes, many of our Lord's disciples refusing to walk any more with him. 'This is a hard saying,' they complained, 'Who can listen to it?' A saying can be hard in two ways: either hard to understand or difficult to accept – perhaps even both.

Saint Peter spoke up for the smaller group who remained with Jesus. Our Lord's saying was not easier or clearer for him than for those who complained. The difference was that Saint Peter did not complain; he believed, and accepted it in advance. The others did not believe: their capacity to believe had been eaten away by that cancer of the soul, habitual murmuring and complaint against God.

And what was the saying that split the disciples so dramatically into two groups: one which remained aloof and alien to Christ to this day, the Jewish people, and the other which gradually grew into the Christian Church? It was our Lord's saying 'my flesh is food indeed, and my blood is drink indeed . . he who eats this bread will live forever.'

A great change had to take place in our Lord himself, before his flesh and blood were available as food and drink. He had to ascend where he was before: from being a body that could be crucified, and blood that could be shed, he had to become flesh and blood no longer under the power of death. He was to be crucified in weakness, but he lives by the power of God.

Here at Mass, a great change has to take place in the bread and wine by consecration, before they are available to us as the body and blood of Christ. Let us stand firm with Saint Peter, and accept what we do not understand. Let us pray that the bread and wine changed into the body and blood of Christ, will change us too, so that we become available to Christ for his purposes for us.

72 Ephphatha — Adaperire
Sunday 23, Year B

What we hear and what we say, *how* we hear and *how* we speak, determine to a great extent what we do, and eventually make us what we are.

The whole human race resembles the deaf mute in today's Gospel. We all need the healing, creating hand of Christ to make us hear and speak aright: we need to call on the Son of God, to pray that he who formed man from clay in the beginning, would come again and remake the work of his hands. This is what the Church sings in Advent:

> O King of the nations, whom all the peoples desire,
> you are the cornerstone which makes both nations one.
> O come and save man
> whom you made from clay. (*Daily Prayer,* 63).

We know that when Christ our King comes again, he will not be swayed by disputing tongues, nor by the plotting of men, we know that

> He shall not decide by what his eyes see,
> or decide by what his ears hear;
> but with righteousness he shall judge the poor
> and decide with equity for the meek of the earth.
>
> (Is.11:3-4, RSVCE)

'It were my soul's desire to imitate my King.' Each of us has to learn to hear and speak as the prophet foretold of Jesus:

> The Lord God has given me
> the tongue of a teacher
> and skill to console the weary
> The Lord God opened my ears
> and I did not disobey or turn back in defiance. (Is.50:4-5, NEB)

To have an ear that is attuned each morning to God's ever-renewed message; to have a tongue that can encourage the faint-hearted: this indeed will be to have one's ears opened and one's tongue unloosed. Then each of us will be able to praise Christ our Lord, saying: He has done all things well; he has made the deaf to hear and the dumb to speak.

73 Christo Vero Regi
Sunday 24, Year B

Saint Benedict, addressing anyone who wishes to become a monk, asks him to renounce his own wishes, and take up the 'tough, shining weapons of obedience,' and serve as a soldier under the Lord Christ, the true King. In looking on our Lord as a warrior King, engaged in war, and on Christians as soldiers in his army, St Benedict is echoing the feeling of the early centuries of Christianity, the times in which he lived.

Perhaps today's Gospel offers a different image of Christ: a defeated, not a victorious King. The basic question for us all which our Lord put to the apostles: 'whom do you say the Son of Man is?' We are in danger of watering down our image of Christ, so that he becomes one leader among many, one voice in the crowd, the founder of one possible religion among the world religions, no longer Christ the Victorious King as St Benedict saw him.

To pray to our Lord as to our King, is to be quite clear that to him belong the seasons and the centuries, that he will come again in glory to judge the living and the dead, and that his kingdom will have no end.

> The kings of Sheba and Seba
> shall bring him gifts.
> Before him all kings shall fall prostrate,
> all nations shall serve him. (Ps 71: 9-11)

Why then did our Lord begin to teach them that 'the Son of Man must suffer many things, and be rejected by the elders and the chief priests and the scribes, and be killed.' (Mk.8:31)

It was because he was engaged in a mysterious kind of war, he was bringing a deeper kind of peace which this world cannot give. He was to struggle with death itself, and prove his kingship by rising from the dead, by ascending into heaven, by sending down the Holy Spirit, by converting the nations, and by forming his Church to be a visible kingdom on earth.

If we do not see clear evidence that our Lord is winning his war against the powers of evil, we must, nevertheless, as good soldiers of Christ Jesus, take our share of hardship, looking forward in hope to the glorious coming of our Saviour. 'Behold he is coming in the clouds, and every eye will see him, every one who pierced him.' (Apoc 1:7)

95

74 They were afraid to ask him
Sunday 25, Year B

The apostles did not understand what Jesus was saying to them, and they were afraid to ask him.

There are many things happening in the Church of Christ today, which we do not understand, and like the apostles we are afraid to ask Jesus the meaning of them.

We see authority flouted, doctrines questioned, people perplexed. We see open conflict within the Church. What is the meaning of all this? How has it happened? Where will it end?

Let us not be afraid to ask our Lord for the answers. He has already told us many of the answers in his own words in the Gospel.

Is the Church divided? He has compared the Church to a field in which corn and weeds are growing: the weeds will be eventually burned up; the corn will be stored away. He compared the Church to a trawler's net, catching all kinds of fish: the catch is eventually sorted out, and only what is good is retained. He has warned us that some teachers will come in his name, looking like sheep on the outside, but inside they are really wild wolves.

The Church then is not the final word of God's dealings with mankind: it is a field, a net in which God's work is in progress. Within that field and that net, each of us has to co-operate with God's work, in fear and trembling, as Saint Paul tells us, working out our salvation. (Phil 2:12).

'Do not let your heart be distressed, neither let it play the coward' was our Lord's message to the apostles, when he foretold all these things. (Jn 14:27 Knox)

He has given us an easy rule by which to distinguish the corn from the weeds, the sheep from the wolves, the good catch in the net from the bad. You will know them by the way they act. A healthy tree cannot bear bad fruit, and a poor tree cannot bear good fruit.

'Forewarned is forearmed' the proverb says. The great Italian poet, Dante said the same thing in different words: 'The arrow that is seen coming, wounds less.'

75 Ejice Eum
Sunday 26, Year B

Our Lord invites us to enter into life crippled, lame, and with the sight of only one eye, if we wish to be saved. He is really telling us of the restraints we have to put on our hands, our feet and our eyes if we wish to 'keep ourselves unstained from the world.'

(James 1:27)

This is the psalmist's prayer:
    He rewarded me because I was just,
    repaid me, for *my hands were clean,*
    for I have kept the way of the Lord
    and have not fallen away from my God. (Ps.17:21-2)
And again:
    Keep my eyes from what is false:
    by your word give me life. (Ps.118:37)
And again, in St. Luke's Gospel:
    . . . the day shall dawn upon us from on high . . .
    to guide *our feet* into the way of peace. (1:78-9)

Our two hands, our two feet, our two eyes: these are three double fountains of life, bubbling all day long. In our day, it is our eyes, above all, which are in constant motion, ceaselessly besieged on all sides by our highly visual culture.

And it is at this point that our Lord's warning sounds: ' . . . if your eye should cause you to sin, tear it out.' We do not need to suspect that evil is lurking in everything that we see or look at. On the other hand, it would be unrealistic to ignore the fact that the modern world tries to entice our curiosity – often a dangerous curiosity – by the way it offers us to look at and experience life.

What are we to do, as Christians in this situation? St. Paul gives us the answer: We do not need to go out of the world, but:

    Do not be overcome by evil,
    but overcome evil by good. (Rom.12:21)

76 Spiritual Sonship
Sunday 27, Year B

Even the youngest boy in the school has already outgrown his childhood. What is true in his case, is even more true of all the others present here. We cannot, we have not, remained children. How can we do what our Lord says in today's Gospel: 'whoever does not receive the kingdom of God like a child shall not enter it.' We cannot remain children.

If we cannot remain children, perhaps we can retain something of childhood? Yes indeed, and Saint Paul urges us, 'Keep the innocence of children, with the thoughts of grown men.' (1 Cor. 14:20, Knox) To preserve the innocence of childhood into boyhood and beyond is a great grace. But it is not the whole of what our Lord means here: it is only a step on the way.

We outgrow each successive stage in life, but one thing we can never outgrow.

We never can outgrow our sonship as children of God. Ultimately we depend on God: we must not conceal this fact from ourselves. Our better self will acknowledge it in the secret of our own heart, in our better moments.

Our great task in the Christian life is to keep this dependence on God always before our minds. Since life itself is God's gift to us, all we are and have should be his. This is what St. Benedict calls humility. It is what we are tempted to rebel against.

Our great temptation is disobedience to God's rule or kingdom: we resent having to accept his rule 'as a little child.'

The psalmist underwent this struggle, and found peace when he surrendered to God's rule:

> O Lord, my heart is not proud
> nor haughty my eyes.
> I have not gone after things too great
> nor marvels beyond me.

> Truly I have set my soul
> in silence and peace.
> A weaned child on its mother's breast
> even so is my soul.

hope in the Lord, both now and for ever. (Ps. 130)

77 In Toto Corde

Sunday 31, Year B

Did Israel listen? Do we listen? Certainly many in Israel did listen, and loved God with all their heart, with all their soul, with all their mind and with all their strength. The psalmist spoke of their listening and loving when he prayed in his own name and theirs:

> O God, you are my God, for you I long;
> for you my soul is thirsting.
> My body pines for you
> like a dry weary land without water.
> So I gaze on you in the sanctuary
> to see your strength and your glory. (Ps 62:2-3)

Do we listen? Yes certainly, but perhaps we listen more to the second than to the first commandment. The newer generation among us takes the needs of others more to heart, is more willing to do something practical for their neighbour. And above all, it should not be a substitute for, nor an escape from, the commandment to love God for his own sake, with all one's heart.

'Where your treasure is, there will your heart be also.'

If God is our treasure, then our heart will naturally turn to think of him, a hundred times a day, unconsciously, without effort. Our Lord desires that we should love him, that we may be eternally saved, and desires that we may be saved that we may love him eternally. (St Francis de Sales, *Treatise on the Love of God,* Bk II, ch. VIII.) He says: 'I am come to cast fire on the earth; and what will I but that it be kindled.' God the Father had said long before: 'Be converted, do penance, return to me, live, why dost thou die, O house of Israel.'

> Likewise the Spirit helps us in our weakness; for we do not know hw to pray as we ought, but the Spirit himself intercedes for us with sighs too deep for words. (Rom 8:26)

May our God, Father, Son and Holy Spirit, the Blessed and undivided Trinity, bring us all alike to everlasting life, to see his strength and his glory.

78 Gratitude

Sunday 31, Year B

Our Lord asks us to make room in our lives for God. The easiest way for us to make room in our lives for someone else is to remember. The psalmist says this when he says to God:

> I remember the days gone by;
> I think about all that you have done,
> I bring to mind all your deeds. (Ps.143:5. TEV)

Gratitude to God will expand our mind, our soul, our heart. It will smother our complaints, and change our bad moods to contentment. It will make room for God in our lives.

> The thought of God, and nothing short of it, is the happiness of man . . . He alone is sufficient for the heart who made it . . . Life passes . . . popularity is fickle, the senses decay, the world changes, friends die. One alone is constant; one alone is true to us; one alone can be all things to us. (Newman, *Parochial and Plain Sermons,* V, 316,326).

Gratitude to God will grow into love for God, love of him with all our heart, and with all our soul, and with all our mind, and with all our strength.

> How can we delight in the Lord if he is far away from us? But take care that he is not far away. You are the one who makes him far away. Love, and he will come near; love, and he will dwell with you. 'The Lord is at hand. Have no anxiety about anything.' (St. Augustine, *The Divine Office,* 3,775).

And what of our neighbour? We have to make room for our many neighbours in our own life. Our Lord means by 'neighbour' not just the person next door, nor our own relatives merely, nor again does he mean our 'fellowman' in a vague, general sense, so common today. The neighbour our Lord asks us to love is the one who at this moment most needs our help.

Our love for God is mainly one of gratitude; our love for our neighbour, one of compassion.

If we follow out this twofold commandment, Jesus will say to us as to the scribe: 'You are not far from the kingdom of God.'

79 Duo Minuta Quod Est Quadrans

Sunday 32, Year B

I suppose we all feel instictively the difference between a photograph and a painting. Once looked at, the photograph is filed away in an album; but we hang the painting on the wall of the room: it is our companion, year in, year out, When the painting is a portrait, it invites us to reflect and to discover family resemblances in the person portrayed.

The Gospel we have just heard paints a lasting portrait. Out of all the procession of people placing their offerings in the Temple treasury, it picks out the widow who put in two small coins, the equivalent of a penny.

There is a family resemblance between this widow, and that other widow who fed the prophet for three years 'from the jar of meal and jug of oil.' Both offerings were small, but decisive.

Nobody gives as much as those who hold nothing back for themselves. (St. Ambrose, *De Viduis* V,27).

We all have something more important than money to offer to God in worship.

First of all our total attention when we are here at Mass. God loves a cheerful giver. Let us give cheerfully, without holding anything back, of our time and attention to what is going on at the altar; in the readings; in the singing; in our praying the Creed together.

Secondly, our right intention. The choir and the monks are not here just to stage a performance, neither do you come merely to view a spectacle. We are all still under the eye of Jesus, just as the procession in the Temple was. He is still looking for the secret places of our heart, where our deep decisions are made. As he sees us, let us in turn try to see him with the eyes of our heart: let us offer him our two small coins of attention and intention as a token of our willingness to be judged by him alone at the end.

80 Nazareth

Sunday 4, Year C

The whole point of today's Gospel is that it took place at *Nazareth*. Nazareth was our Lady's village: it was here that 'the angel Gabriel was sent by God to a virgin betrothed to a man named Joseph, of the house of David.'

After the finding of our Lord in the temple when he was twelve years old he 'went back with them to Nazareth, where he was obedient to them . . . Jesus grew both in body and in wisdom, gaining favour with God and men.' (Lk.2:51-52, TEV)

What happened now to this favour he had had with the men of Nazareth? How did it come about that the people of his own village were filled with anger to such a point that they dragged him out of the synagogue, intending to throw him over the cliff?

It was not his person, but his mission which came between him and them. They could not accept him for more than what they knew of him: 'They said: Isn't he the son of Joseph?' In their eyes there was to be no mystery to them, no revelation in him.

Once Jesus began to speak as a prophet, the jealousy blinded their eyes. The words of God in his mouth as a prophet stung them to jealousy. It was like what we heard about the prophet Jeremiah in the first reading of today's Mass:

> Stand up and tell them
> all I command you.
> Do not be dismayed at their presence . . .
> I, for my part, today will make you
> into a fortified city,
> a pillar of iron,
> and a wall of bronze
> to confront all this land . . .
> They will fight against you
> but shall not overcome you . . .

At the end of our Lord's life it was still the same: St. Matthew tells us that Pilate 'knew very well that the Jewish authorities had handed Jesus over to him because they were jealous.' (Mt.27:18, TEV)

As it was with Jesus, so it is with his Church.

81 In Captura Piscium
Sunday 5, Year C

Jesus showed himself to be a better fisherman than Peter. Peter had eyes only for his soiled nets and empty boat; he could not see that Jesus too was fishing. Peter was blind to the crowds pressing into Jesus' net to be saved. Peter was engrossed in his own work, to earn a living; he did not yet share Jesus' work, to offer salvation.

I admire our Lord's tact. He wants to have Peter at his side, to share in his work for people, and leave fishing to others. But he does not make any direct assault on Peter's freedom, nor force him to open his eyes to see God's work awaiting him. No, first he asks a favour: 'Getting into one of the boats which was Simon's, he asked him to put out a little from the land.' (Lk 5:3) Next, he offers the tempting bait: 'Put out into the deep and let down your nets for a catch.' It was Peter's obedience to this word, this call, which hooked him. There was no going back: 'And when they brought their boats to land, they left everything' – including the miraculous draught of fish, which was now superfluous – 'and followed him.'

'From age to age you gather a people to yourself.' And from age to age, Jesus calls others to share his work, filling the places left by the death of each preceding generation.

Our age is privileged to see Peter at his new work of netting people for Christ, in a way and an extent which surpasses perhaps the action of any single one of his successors up to now. Pope John Paul is proving himself a mighty fisherman at this task. And just as Jesus caught Saint Peter for his work, in the middle of Peter's own work – and even in a moment of disappointment 'Master, we toiled all night and took nothing! But at your work I will let down the nets,' so our present Pope goes straight to our daily problems of family life in order to help us 'to recapture the ultimate meaning of life and its fundamental values.' Let us stay with him to follow Christ.

Ag Críost an síol, 7rl.

82 Martha and Mary
Sunday 16, Year C

Every single word or deed of our Lord's is complete in itself. Any action, any saying, any reply of his contains a law of life in germ. It is afterwards developed by the Church, as each generation keeps the Gospel ever before its eyes as a code of divine truth.

In the Gospel about Martha and Mary, our Lord has something important to say to us. He is not speaking here about the difference between what is good and what is bad, but between what is good and what is better.

Martha's complaint was made on the spur of the moment, but undoubtedly it only brought to the surface the judgment she had already made on her sister. Her fault did not lie in being upset. Our Lord overlooks this, he even soothes her by repeating her name twice as a sign of affectionate understanding: Martha, Martha . . . Her fault lay in judging her sister. This is the deep lesson we must take from the story: not to judge others; and further, to realize that the others have their place in God's plan, just as they are.

This was precisely Martha's mistake. If the hospitality of the two sisters was to consist only in preparing the meal, who was to do the other side of hospitality: entertain the guest, speak to him, and in this case more important still, listen to him?

The Lord did not blame Martha's work, but he distinguished between the services the two sisters rendered him. 'Be still and know that I am God' was Mary's service, the better part that would not be taken from her.

There is a parallel scene in Saint John's Gosepl, and a similar reply of our Lord's:

> Peter turned and saw following them the disciple whom Jesus loved, who had lain close to his breast at the supper and had said 'Lord, who is it that is going to betray you?' When Peter saw him he said to Jesus, 'Lord, what about this man?' Jesus said to him, 'What is that to you? Peter had been given his own task 'Feed my lambs, feed my sheep.' John was to be led to other pastures where 'In the beginning was the Word, and the Word was with God, and the Word was God.'

This is the Word Mary was listening to, as she sat at the feet of Jesus.

83 The Narrow Door

Sunday 21, Year C

'Strive to enter by the narrow door.' The door is narrow, and the way it leads out to is also narrow. It is the narrow way of life.

Our Lord had been asked: 'Lord, will those who are saved be few?' He did not answer directly whether they would be few or many. What he did say was that the door to salvation was narrow and 'many will seek to enter and will not be able.'

Where are we to find that door? It is some secret entrance in each of our lives. It is a point where life seems to narrow down on us, through some trial, some disappointment, some reduction in our importance, some attack of illness, some loss of our energy and powers.

We are asked to go through that particular door, and walk the narrow way beyond it, without faltering or grumbling.

The psalmist expressed our feelings for us:

> And so when my heart grew embittered
> and when I was cut to the quick,
> I was stupid and did not understand,
> no better than a beast in your sight.
> Yet I was always in your presence;
> you were holding me by my right hand.
> You will guide me by your counsel
> and so you will lead me to glory.
> What else have I in heaven but you
> Apart from you I want nothing on earth. (Ps 72:21-25).

The trials of life are not so much a punishment for sin as a purification for heaven. They narrow us down to one particular door at some particular stage in our life, but they bring us all the faster to the next stage where God is waiting for us. Let us then, as we heard in the second Reading, 'Therefore lift your drooping hands and strengthen your weak knees . . . Strive for peace with all men and for the holiness without which no one will see the Lord.'

84 To return to ourselves
Sunday 24, Year C

The three parables we have just heard once again speak to us of God's great mercy for those who sin and turn away from him; those who are lost. God is good to those who do not sin and who remain loyal to him, as did the elder brother, but his merciful love for the returned prodigal has something more expansive about it. In the same way to find the missing sheep and the lost coin, is to restore the one to the sheepfold, the other to the woman's purse; it rounds out the number of the sheep and the amount of the money.

The third parable, that of the conversion of the prodigal son, is particularly useful for us in this year 1983, which the Holy Father has called the anniversary of the year A.D. 33, the traditional year of our Lord's death.

We are invited in a special way this year to make greater use of the sacrament of Penance, of reconciliation. Here we see the inner truth of how to go about it, not merely by exterior compulsion, but by an inner sincerity and real sorrow for what we have done.

First of all to *return to ourselves.* We sin by forgetting the true purpose of life; who we are; why we are here; how long more we shall be here. Let us return to ourselves. Then say 'I will arise *and go to my Father.'* We do this by coming to Church, to where God has lodged the power of forgiving sins in his name: to the ordained priest. Finally, to come to the moment of truth, and *accuse ourselves* in all simplicity and sincerity, without excuses.

God's kindness comes to meet us more than half-way.

> As a father has compassion on his sons,
> the Lord has pity on those who fear him;
> for he knows of what we are made,
> he remembers that we are dust. (Ps 102:13-14)

What a pity that people avail themselves less than they used to of God's grace awaiting them in the sacrament of forgiveness. His grace and mercy are waiting for us there; all we have to do is to return to ourselves, to arise and come to our Father, ask his forgiveness and receive abundant peace for our heart and soul.

85 Dives and Lazarus
Sunday 26, Year C

When the thought of eternal punishment comes home to us as a possibility, it fills us with dread. The subject is avoided today; the style even of popular missions has changed; hell is hardly mentioned.

Our Lord speaks of it quite clearly in today's parable. The story is a parable, not an actual account of two men who actually existed. But the setting of the story is real: on the one hand, paradise (the bosom of Abraham), on the other hell. And between them there is no road or bridge by which to pass.

'Eternal punishment is the only true measure of the guilt of sin.' People today call sin by soft names. They explain it away. 'The world laughs at it, and is indulgent to it; and as to its deserving eternal punishment, it rises up indignant at the idea, and rather than admit it, would deny the God who has said it does.' (Newman, *Meditations and Devotions,* Part III, IV. 3 & 4, 2nd edn., 1893, 460, 462).

Our Lord does not elaborate on the reasons why the rich man was condemned to hell. Besides his selfishness in living with a poor man at his gate, a poor man whom he ignored, his guilt lay in not listening to what Moses and the prophets could have taught him about how to live in order to please God.

Abraham says it would be useless to send someone from the dead to convert the five brothers of the rich man: if they would not practise what they already knew, they would refuse to believe another prophet.

In our own case, we know from the Gospel what we have to do. We are better off than the rich man, because some one has come back from death to help us to avoid hell and reach heaven. Jesus himself is our guide, our shepherd through life.

86 To look Death daily in the Face
Sunday 26, Year C

Our Lord himself has spoken to us just now through the words of the Gospel about eternal reward and eternal punishment. The saints have echoed his words: Saint Paul tells us: 'Keep on working with fear and trembling to complete your salvation because God is always at work in you to make you willing and able to obey his own purpose.' (Phil.2:12,13, TEV) And Saint Benedict urges his followers to 'fear the Day of Judgment; to dread hell; to desire eternal life with all spiritual longing; to keep death daily before one's eyes.' (Rule c.4)

This is not morbid advice. Our Lord, Saint Paul, Saint Benedict are only asking us to get used to the great coming fact for each of us. We are all walking along a thousand different roads towards the gates of death. Once we have passed through those gates, there will be, ultimately, only two different destinations. In today's Gospel, our Lord speaking to the Jewish Pharisees, used words with which they as Jews were familiar to describe these destinations: happiness in the bosom of Abraham, sadness in Hades. Elsewhere in the Gospel he uses other images, more familiar, perhaps, to us: on the one hand, his Father's house, on the other, the outer darkness.

As each of us pases through those gates of death, earth will fade away behind us. We shall discover 'that great and solemn truth' when 'we stand before God in judgment, that to us there are but two beings in the whole world, God and ourselves . . . Every one will have to think of himself . . . every one will be rendering to him his own account. By thinking of it beforehand we hope to mitigate its terrors when it comes . . . (Newman, *Sermons on Subjects of the Day*, 1891, 38-9).

In the meantime, let us make our own one of the loveliest of the Church's prayers for the dead:
God of mercy and power
whose Son of his own free will
underwent a human death on our behalf:
let us, your children,
share in the victory of Christ's resurrection.
We ask this through Christ our Lord. (Cf. *Daily Prayer*, 527*).

87 Fallaces Divitiae

Sunday 26, Year C

Nothing is so disappointing as money, and few things prevent us from thinking seriously about religion so much as a constant concern for money, whether we have little or much.

The psalmist said it long ago:

> You have given me a short span of days
> my life is as nothing in your sight.
> A mere breath, the man who stood so firm,
> a mere shadow, the man passing by,
> a mere breath the riches he hoards,
> not knowing who will have them. (Ps 38:6-7)

Times are getting hard once again: the signs of the times point to the rapid disappearance of affluence and the return of hardship, even of poverty, for many families. We are being thrown back into a situation where once again prayer for God's help in our difficulties seems more easy to accept. We can all make our own the beautifully resigned prayer in the Book of Proverbs:

> Give me neither poverty nor wealth, provide me only with the food I need.
> If I have too much, I shall deny thee and say, 'Who is the Lord?'
> If I am reduced to poverty, I shall steal and blacken the name of God. (Prov. 30:8)

Today's Gospel is a warning by our Lord: the rich man's brothers would not believe Moses and the prophets, neither would they believe if our Lord himself rose from the dead. Their wealth dragged them down to earth and choked heaven out of sight.

We have of course our duty to get on in life, and to get on with life. But our Lord asks us to remain detached from money as the measure of life. Where your treasure is, there will your heart be also. If our only treasure is money, what will our heart feed on when it is our turn to be 'a mere shadow the man passing by, a mere breath the riches he hoards not knowing who will have them.'

88 Unprofitable Servants
Sunday 27, Year C

Our Lord takes for granted in the Gospel the hard life of a slave in ancient times. His listeners were familiar with it also; to plough all day, to serve at the Master's table at night; the point our Lord is making is because it was an accepted fact on all sides, he wants us to look on our work for God in the same light.

Having ploughed all day in the field, there will be still some further task for each of us to do in the evening of life. Lighter work of course, not the ploughing in the field, but still some service for the Lord, before we can finally sit down to rest.

This may seem a harsh way of dealing with us, to work us till the end, but God is greater than our heart and knows all things. He knows that if we think and talk too long about any task we have just completed, we will spoil it by taking credit for it to ourselves. We would forget his supporting and rewarding hand. If we leave the work to him, the field that we have ploughed will yield an eternal harvest.

As we round off each successive stage in life, we should place it in God's hands. Saint Paul says somewhere:

> . . . it is by God's grace that you have been saved through faith. It is not the result of your own efforts, but God's gift, so that no one can boast about it. God has made us what we are and in our union with Christ Jesus he has created us for a life of good deeds, which he has already prepared for us to do. (Eph.2:8-10, TEV)

Throughout our life then, from youth on, we should be able to disengage from each completed task with detachment, and say:

> Not to us Lord, not to us,
> but to your name give the glory
> for the sake of your love and your truth. (Ps. 113B:1).

When old age comes, we shall find some further, final work to do for the Master, no longer in the harsh outdoor conditions of the long day, but something more equal to our declining forces.

> While I said I have toiled in vain,
> I have spent my strength for nothing,
> and all the while my cause was with the Lord,
> my recompense with my God. (Is.49:4)

89 In Domo Tua Oportet Me Manere
Sunday 31, Year C

In life the tiniest things are bound up with the greatest; a simple gesture, the action of a moment has power within itself to change the whole course of a life. And so, Saint Luke has caught with an artist's eye, and fixed for all time, the spontaneous action of Zacchaeus: we still see him, as all preceding Christian centuries have seen him, throw dignity to the winds, and climb up that tree in order to see Jesus pass.

> O Lord, you search me and you know me,
> you know my resting and my rising,
> you discern my purpose from afar,
> you mark when I walk or lie down,
> all my ways lie open to you. (Ps. 138, Grail)

Zacchaeus 'made haste and came down, and received him joyfully.' But he did not receive Jesus as one might receive an accidental guest; he opened up to the Lord, not only his house, but his conscience and his heart. While those around him argued and complained, he, in all simple sincerity declared to the Lord what would be his life from now on: 'Behold, Lord, the half of my goods I give to the poor; and if I have defrauded anyone of anything, I restore it fourfold.'

This is what Jesus meant when he said: 'Today salvation has come to this house.' Salvation came, when the Saviour was enthroned in the householder's conscience; he gives himself over to God in the person of Jesus, and considers himself his servant henceforth.

The peculiar character of our Lord's goodness, as displayed in this incident, is its tenderness and considerateness for each individual. This is its message to us here today. God has a 'Particular Providence' for each one of us in Jesus. Let us acknowledge Jesus as enthroned within us at the very springs of thought and affection. We are his house. Let us submit ourselves to his guidance and sovereign direction; let us come to him that he may forgive us, cleanse us, change us, guide us, and save us.

90 Stay with us, Lord Jesus, as Evening falls

Sunday 31, Year C

Zacchaeus ran ahead to free himself from the crowd, the better to be able to see Jesus. Unknown to himself, it was his whole former life, and not just curiosity which urged him on. In spite of having the handling of much money, and of being himself a rich man, he had always obeyed God's law of justice: he was good to the poor, and scrupulous in making restitution. He had only heard of Jesus; but now his habitual obedience to conscience was to lead him to obedience to Jesus' Gospel. 'Today salvation has come to this house, since he also is a son of Abraham.'

Jesus offered him salvation, something over and above Zacchaeus' fidelity to justice.

We, as born Catholics, are in almost the opposite situation to Zacchaeus. We have heard of Jesus and his salvation, at the same time as, or even long before, we had the handling of money, or were faced with problems of fair dealing between man and man.

This is perhaps the root of all our social troubles in Ireland today. It is distressing to hear about, let alone, share the burden of all the disputes. As a nation, we know all about the Gospel, but on the whole, again as a nation, can we honestly say with Zacchaeus: 'Behold, Lord, the half of my goods I give to the poor; and if I have defrauded anyone of anything, I restore it fourfold.'

A further danger would be, that in striving to be just and honest men, we might reject the whole teaching of the Gospel, as if somehow it favoured the growth of hypocrisy. No, Jesus is our great way of life. Today's Gospel has given us a glimpse of him as the Way, on the way, the Son of man who had nowhere to lay his head, and who accepts hospitality while conferring salvation. Let us make our own the lovely prayer:

> Stay with us, Lord Jesus, as evening falls:
> be our companion on our way.
> In your mercy inflame our hearts and raise our hope,
> so that, in union with our brethren,
> we may recognize you in the scriptures,
> and in the breaking of Bread. (*Daily Prayer*, [384])

Eight Feast Days

91 In Fear and Trembling

St Patrick's Day

At practically every Mass we attend, we hear a Reading from St. Paul. His letters, difficult indeed as they are at times, still last on, and have been heard in every Christian generation since his day. In this respect St. Paul was more fortunate in his letters than in his foundations: the churches to which he wrote have long since ceased to exist, the countries are in large measure no longer Christian, many of the great cities have vanished; their site now marked by a few sand dunes.

Things are almost exactly the opposite with our apostle, St Patrick. His writings, beautiful indeed as they are, remain a dead letter for most people. But his work lasts on. We can span the centuries almost, between his day and ours by three monuments which are within walking distance of my monastery: the Mass rock of the penal days; the Cistercian monastery in pre-reformation Abington and the ruins of the pre-Norman church in Clonkeen.

St Paul and St Patrick match off almost exactly in character: at a distance they seem like giants, formidable men of granite; from nearby we see them full of anxiety and fears over their flock.

If St Paul's foundations were not preserved for him by God, there is no guarantee that St Patrick's will be either.

We must rid ourselves of the illusion that we are the chosen people whom God cannot reject. This was a central theme in St Paul's life: the anxious mystery of God's rejection of the Jews, the original 'chosen people.' Other races were grafted on to the tree where branches had been lopped off. 'Observe,' he says, 'the kindness and the severity of God – severity to those who fell away, divine kindness to you, if only you remain within its scope.'

(Rom.11:22, NEB)

You must work out your own salvation in fear and trembling; for it is God who works in you, inspiring both the will and the deed, for his own chosen purpose. (Phil.2:12, NEB)

92 Reconciliation

St Patrick's Day

Christianity in Ireland started because one man was able to forgive his enemies, and bring about reconciliation between himself and them. Patrick the prisoner and slave returned to Ireland as Patrick the missionary bishop, bringing the Gospel of Christ to our country. Patrick's forgiveness of his enemies is, under God's providence, the rock on which our particular church is built. The building, to be sound, should be in continuity with its foundations. We know only too well how damaged the fabric of our public and private life is at present by our national inability to forgive and be reconciled with one another.

Here then is a clear and tangible task for each of us on this St Patrick's Day.

In one of his epistles, Saint Paul, writing to the Christians in Corinth, says in the same breath: '. . . We are God's fellow workers; you are God's field, God's building.' (1 Cor.3:9, RSV)

If we look on ourselves as God's field, let us begin today to sow the seeds of peace and reconciliation in our own little corner of the field, that is to say in our own conscience, in our home and among those with whom we come into contact through our work and life generally. God will harvest our crop in due time.

The kingdom of God is like a man who scatters seed in his field. He sleeps at night, is up and about during the day, and all the while the seeds are sprouting and growing. Yet he does not know how it happens. The soil itself makes the plants grow and bear fruit: first the tender stalk appears, then the head, and finally the head full of grain. When the grain is ripe the man starts working with his sickle, for harvest time is come. (Mark 4:26 TEV).

93 Baptism and Conscience
St Patrick's Day

What lies ahead for Irish Catholicism between this and the turn of the new century? Two great areas of concern lie in wait for us: The Infant Baptism of Irish children; the Christian conscience of Irish adolescents and adults.

In the years ahead, there may well be pressures on parents to delay baptism as if baptism compromised the child's freedom to choose its own religion for itself. Baptism however is not a form of religious slavery or constraint but the admittance into true freedom. The results would be disastrous for the Catholic Church in Ireland.

We are so accustomed to baptizing children soon after birth, that we may overlook or neglect what needs to be done for the child when 'consciousness and freedom awake' in the child. Baptism gives a new birth; but the eventual growth in grace and enlightenment needs to be carefully fostered. A so-called neutral attitude on the part of the family with regard to the child's religious life would in fact be a negative choice that would deprive the child of an essential good.

The other great problem will be the Christian conscience of adolescents and adults. Conscience is not identical with self-will: it should act as the echo of a tribunal beyond itself.

Saint Patrick's Day is the feast of our Catholicism rather than of our nationalism: the tradition of the shamrock was meant to illustrate the Three Persons, Father, Son and Holy Spirit, not something to mark off the Irish from the rest of the world. The shamrock is an image of our faith before being an emblem of our nationalism. There may be choices ahead between our religion and our country; between Catholicism and nationalism. May St Patrick pray for the Ireland of today and tomorrow for fidelity to Christ.

94 Silence, Work and Obedience
Saint Joseph's Day

Silence, work and obedience are the three great characteristics of St Joseph: silence in face of an embarrassing and perplexing situation, work to provide for the Mother and Child committed to his care, and obedience to God's direct message to him. (Let us ask pardon for our lack of reserve, our unfinished tasks and our wilful disobedience to God's known will.)

It is curious that the Scripture Reading chosen at the Office of Readings for St Joseph should be taken from the Epistle to the Hebrews in praise of the faith of the Saints of the Old Testament: They did not see the promises which have been revealed to us.

In what sense can St Joseph be numbered among those who had not seen Christianity? Surely no one could have been closer to our Blessed Lord and our Lady.

Perhaps the answer lies in two phrases from St John's Gospel: 'the Spirit was not yet given because Jesus was not yet glorified' and 'Blessed are those who have not seen and have believed.' St Joseph believed before the event; we believe after it. While his privileges were unique, we are, in one sense, given still greater gifts – we are made members of Christ 'bone of his bone' through water and the Holy Spirit.

The further great lesson we can learn from St Joseph's example – and develop it through his intercession – is that our faith has to be exercised not only on the doctrines we believe, but also on the circumstances in which our lot is cast in life. Providence is arranging our lives step by step and we have to be careful to keep in step.

It is for this reason that my own favourite picture of St Joseph is a beautiful medieval mosaic which portrays him with a youngish strong face and eager eyes, and in his hands the two doves to be offered at the Presentation in the Temple. His whole being is concentrated in the present moment to which Providence has led him. he is at his post, intent on doing God's will.

95 Blended in Death

Saints Peter and Paul

There is a beautiful group of small stained glass windows here in our church in honour of St Peter and St Paul. The artist has conveyed the deep lesson of their separate lives: distinct in their vocations and their work, they were blended in their death as martyrs.

That is why we feel somehow that we are celebrating not two saints, but one. But the oneness is that of the completed picture, not that of the individual parts.

The first panel shows our Lord calling Peter who is holding his fishing net. Paul is not there: how could he be? He had no share in the first foundation of the gospel: he was not one of the twelve apostles, even when the number had been brought to completion once again after the death of Judas.

St Peter had become a fisher of men for Christ long before St Paul had even reached the waters of baptism. It was Christ himself from heaven who snatched St Paul out of the life he was living to set him on the unique task that awaited him.

The second panel in the stained glass pictures St Paul being met by St Peter outside Rome when he arrives there as a prisoner. He had laid the foundations of many churches without undertaking the government of any of them. Those who met him outside Rome were already Christians, but not of his making: he had prayed, he told the Romans in his letter to them 'that somehow or other I may succeed at long last in coming to visit you.' He had not anticipated that he would come as a prisoner.

The third panel shows the last embrace of the two apostles as they prepare for death. Two magnificent churches in Rome cover the last resting place of the two apostles. Even here that blending of differences in unity may be felt. The ribbed dome of St Peter's seashell pink against the blue Roman sky is familiar to us all from a thousand photographs: it is seldom empty. Usually it is thronged with pilgrims and sightseers. The vast cool interior of St Paul's is not so well known to those who live outside Rome, and even in Rome itself it is seldom filled with crowds. But both churches speak to us of the two apostles, called by Christ in different ways, labouring in different provinces, emphasizing different aspects of the one, true, apostolic faith, blended in death as they shed their blood for Christ.

96 Disagreements
Saint Barnabas

Nothing is more distressing in life than disagreements; no disagreements go deeper and last longer than disagreements over a third person.

This was St Barnabas' great cross in life. Everything St Luke tells us about Barnabas in the Acts suggests a harmonious, gentle, encouraging person, one dedicated to a priestly way of life even before he became a Christian. His very name 'Barnabas' was a nickname given to him by the apostles meaning 'son of consolation.'

The Holy Spirit said, 'I must have Barnabas and Saul dedicated to the work to which I have called them.' St Paul's character and conversion had something fierce and abrupt about it, and I find it hard not to see him guilty of 'grieving the Holy Spirit' in his subsequent quarrel with and separation from Barnabas.

Their difference was not about the faith, nor even about the divisive subject of the circumcision (here they both saw alike that what was Jewish in the Old Law was not to be imposed on new converts). They quarrelled about a third person, John Mark.

And Barnabas was for taking John, also called Mark, with them. But Paul said: here was a man who left them when they reached Pamphylia, and took no part in the work; it was not right to admit such a man to their company. So sharp was their disagreement, that they separated from each other; Barnabas took Mark with him and sailed off for Cyprus, while Paul chose Silas for his companion and went on his journey . . .

(Acts 15:37-40 Knox)

St Paul subsequently outstripped and outshone Barnabas in the eyes of history. Barnabas, the wronged party in the dispute, the 'son of consolation' was as it were pushed into second place. St Paul was given time in his own long imprisonments to hone down the rough edges of his somewhat fiery zeal.

97 Virginity and Wisdom
Saint Columba

'The year is the symbol of eternity, for it continually turns round on itself and never comes to rest.' (*The Divine Office*, 2,509). And the year brings back the feastdays of the saints: the Church brings along the whole of her history each year in the feastdays of the saints.

What she singles out for imitation and invocation in each saint are those particular gifts and graces which mark off the spiritual portrait of each. On Pentecost Sunday we invoked the Holy Spirit for his 'sevenfold' gifts – it would be truer to say they are a thousand fold; each of the saints is, so to say, a different mix.

Today is the feast of St Columba, secondary patron of Ireland and in a special way, patron of Glenstal.

The two graces which the Church singles out in St Columba are virginity and wisdom, Christian virginity and Christ's wisdom, that is a special love of Christ and a docility to the Holy Spirit. The counterparts in the natural order are purity and intelligence. In the Christian soul these natural gifts are raised through Baptism to a higher reality and centred on the person of the Son of God in love, and the person of the Holy Spirit in wisdom.

The saints cannot give us by their own power a share in their gifts, but they can pray for us; they make special intercessions for the graces in which they themselves – through the Spirit – excelled. Let us pray this day to St Columba for that wisdom which St. James has described for us.

> . . . the wisdom that comes down from above is essentially something pure; it also makes for peace, and is kindly and considerate; it is full of compassion and shows itself by doing good; nor is there any trace of partiality or hypocrisy in it. Peacemakers, when they work for peace, sow the seeds which will bear fruit in holiness. (James 3:17,18, JB)

98 Catena Christi
Saint Benedict

When St Benedict lived at Monte Cassino, there was another monk, not of St Benedict's immediate circle, living alone in a cave in the Campania. This good man distrusted his own powers of perseverance in his lonely life, and to prevent himself deserting his post, adopted a drastic remedy. He literally tied himself to a rock by an iron chain, one end of the chain clamped to the rock, the other to one of his own ankles. St Benedict's reaction to the hermit's misguided sense of self-discipline was to send him a message, in a terse Latin phrase: 'Si servus Dei es, non teneat te catena ferri, sed catena Christi.' 'If you are a servant of God, bind yourself with the chain of Christ, not with that chain of iron.'

Now Benedict himself had in his early life also lived alone in a cave, and had on one occasion adopted as drastic a remedy when tempted to desert the wilderness of Subiaco and go back down to the warm, throbbing city life in Rome. Tradition still points out the site of the thorn bush into which he threw himself to conquer the temptation.

What had happened to him in the meantime to turn him away from such violent efforts to safeguard perseverance? he had discovered the chain that bound him to Christ, which bound him more securely than the iron clamp in the rock, subdued his temptations more effectively than the thorn bush.

I think this was the journey Saint Benedict made from youth to age: from accepting the first invitation to friendship offered by Christ, he came gradually to accept the mastery of Christ over his whole life. From walking with the Son of Man alone in the rocky glen of Subiaco, he came to see the power of the Risen Saviour in his sacraments, and to adore Christ the Son of God, in prayer with his community., So, in Subiaco he hardly knew what day of the week or season of the year it was – a visitor told him it was Easter Sunday: Benedict was living apart from men, and almost apart from the sacraments. At the end of life however, his last act was one of communion in the Body and Blood of the Lord, and raising his hands once more in prayer, he died.

Those who follow Saint Benedict's way are invited to make the same discovery of Christ for themselves: from friendship to adoration; from the iron chain and the thorn bush to eating the Flesh and drinking the Blood of the Lord, persevering in prayer and work until He returns in glory.

99 Mass of our Lady
'On Saturday'

In medieval times people loved to find reasons for what they celebrated in the liturgy. Sometimes these reasons may appear fanciful, not to say childish, to us. Nevertheless, on reflection, one often finds a deep understanding of the Christian mystery beneath the surface of their thought.

This Mass of our Lady in Sabbato is a case in point. Five reasons were given, one of them legendary, but two of the others worthy of our attention still. Firstly, Saturday was our Lady's day, because on Holy Saturday, she alone remained full of faith: the faith of the followers of Christ was concentrated in her, while the apostles fled. Secondly, Saturday is the gate to Sunday, the Lord's Day; and so Saturday is our Lady's Day, the gate of heaven.

We might remember all those who have sung this Mass in our monasteries for over a continuous thousand years. The past is not dead, simply because it is over.

Concede . . .
'The joy of constant health of mind and body.' This is the particular grace which the author of today's prayer associated with our Lady's intercession. Not wealth, but health. We know that this prayer has been said on Saturdays ever since the eighth century.

It is significant that the great modern shrines of our Lady, such as Lourdes, continue to put this grace in the first place. Our Lady, under this aspect, is the Health of the Sick, *Salus Infirmorum*.

100 Negotiamini dum Venio

The Assumption of the Blessed Virgin Mary

The mysteries of our faith are entrusted to the Church by Christ our Master; he says to us, one and all, 'Trade with these till I come.' We have to put these mysteries to use; we are not to put them out of sight and thus render them unfruitful; on the contrary we have to make them increase; they have to grow under our hands. They are not to change, but they are to develop and fill our minds.

'Trade with these till I come.' The Catholic Church has ever been noted for her active use of the mysteries of Mary, the Mother of Jesus. Where other Christian bodies reduce the honour paid to Mary, the Catholic Church has always maintained this honour and developed it. She is not silent about Mary: she believes that Mary is the *Virgo Praedicanda*, the Virgin to be proclaimed.

And so today we proclaim the Assumption of our Lady, as we shall hear it expressed in the Preface of this Mass:

> Today the virgin Mother of God was taken up
> into heaven
> to be the beginning and the pattern of the
> Church in its perfection,
> and a sign of hope and comfort for your
> people on their pilgrim way.

She is the beginning and pattern of what we are to become when all our earthly ways shall have come to their journey's end; she is a sign of hope and comfort for us on our pilgrim way through this life. Let us then today make our own the psalmist's prayer:

> I rejoiced when I heard them say:
> 'Let us go to God's house.'
> And now our feet are standing
> within your gates, O Jerusalem. (Ps. 121:1-2).

On today's feast we greet our Lady as the Glory of Jerusalem, the Daughter of Sion. And while we honour her at other times as the Mother of God, the Mother of the Church, perhaps today the true secret of her Assumption is to honour her simply as our sister, as the first disciple of Christ, the most docile follower of the Spirit of God, the purest Daughter of the Light Unapproachable. A great servant of Mary, one who had to overcome his original Protestant reluctance to honour her fully, Cardinal John Henry Newman, has said: 'She must be made to fill the mind, in order to suggest the lesson. When once she attracts our attention, then and not till then, she begins to preach Jesus.' (Newman, *Discourses addressed to Mixed Congregations*, 6th edn., 1881, 351). Christ says to us: These are the mysteries; trade with them till I come.

LITURGICAL INDEX

References to the *number* of each Homily